curtains

Contemporary ideas for simple window treatments

and blinds

Lucinda Ganderton and Ali Watkinson
with photography by Polly Eltes

RYLAND
PETERS
& SMALL

LONDON NEW YORK

Designer Fiona Walker
Junior designer Sarah Walden
Senior editor Sophie Bevan
Location research manager Kate Brunt
Picture and location research Emily Westlake
Production manager Patricia Harrington
Art director Gabriella Le Grazie
Publishing director Alison Starling

Illustrator Lizzie Sanders

First published in 2002
This revised paperback edition
published in 2008 in the UK
by Ryland Peters & Small
20–21 Jockey's Fields
London WC1R 2BW
and in the USA
by Ryland Peters & Small, Inc.
519 Broadway
5th Floor
New York, NY 10012

www.rylandpeters.com

10 9 8 7 6 5 4 3 2 1

ISBN: 978-1-84597-701-6

PRINTED IN CHINA

A CIP record for this book is available from
the British Library.

The hardcover edition of this book was
cataloged as follows by the Library of
Congress:

Ganderton, Lucinda.
  Window Treatments : a source book of
contemporary ideas for simple curtains and
shades / Lucinda Ganderton & Ali
Watkinson ; with photography by Polly Eltes.
    p. cm.
    Includes index.
   ISBN 1 84172 329 0
    1. Draperies. 2. Window shades.
I. Watkinson, Ali. II. Title.
TT390 .G35 2002
747'.3–dc21

2002066755

contents

introduction

At the risk of sounding dramatic, there has been nothing short of a revolution in curtain style over the last few years. While it's not exactly curtains for curtains yet, the formerly incontrovertible rule that window dressings should be heavily gathered, lined and interlined, hung from elaborate tracks or poles, festooned with pelmets and tiebacks, and, in consequence, heinously expensive, has been blown asunder.

A relaxed, contemporary approach now prevails that, quite rightly, questions whether curtains need be gathered at all when a flat panel might do the same job; or whether ugly tracks can be replaced with discrete tension wire. This isn't to say that traditional curtains no longer have a place, just that you might want to reserve them for more formal situations or make them from cheap and cheerful calico, ticking or hessian rather than smart damasks, velvets and silks.

There are still some considerations to bear in mind if you are to make the most of your windows and, consequently, of the room as a whole. The first concerns the primary purpose of your window treatment. How much natural daylight are you prepared to give up? Do you want to maximize or minimize the view, keep the room warm, or simply preserve your privacy? Secondly, assess the merits of your window. If it's a thing of beauty, endeavour to show it off. If it's somewhat lacking, and many are, consider a style that will disguise its defects. Finally, bear in mind the function of the room. A style appropriate for a formal sitting room would probably be impractical in a steamy kitchen, and vice versa. Common sense and lateral thinking will guide you, and may throw up some witty reinterpretations. Bathroom windows might be dressed with practical shower-curtain fabric, while in the bedroom, cosy woollen blankets can be held up with stout clips. The nearest there is to a rule is that anything goes.

opposite In this contemporary bedroom, smart cream damask fabric has been given an informal, ungathered heading. Chic and unfussy, it has the advantage of requiring less fabric than more traditional styles. The twig 'pelmet' adds a witty, natural flourish.

this page Recently, fabrics in natural fibres and colours have come to the fore, but as these examples show, they need not result in plain or boring window treatments. A velvet ribbon trim combined with a triple pleat heading lifts neutral linen curtains above the ordinary. Stunning white-on-white hand-embroidered linen is shown to great advantage in otherwise plain Roman blinds. And unusually proportioned vertical stripes lend a crisply tailored look to blinds at a bay window.

styles

SELECTING FABRICS

WORKING WITH PROPORTIONS

SHEERS

DETAILS

SELECTING FABRICS

The enormous variety of fabrics now available can be mind-bogglingly confusing. However, by imposing some practical limitations you can begin to narrow the field.

Start with the purpose of the room. Is its use predominantly formal or informal? This may influence whether you choose a chic or inexpensive fabric, although even cheap, utilitarian fabrics can look impressive when bedecked with opulent trimmings. Will you need to wash the curtains? This is especially important in kitchens, bathrooms and children's bedrooms, as dry-cleaning curtains can be prohibitively expensive.

Then consider the physical characteristics of the room. Is it sunny or dark? If it's the latter, heavy, dark-coloured fabrics will tend to rob the room of what little light it has, so are best avoided. Is it a cold or warm room? A cosy, richly coloured fabric will warm up a cold room both visually and physically.

Think, too, about your preferred style of window treatment. If you want the fabric to gather in sumptuous folds, choose a medium- to heavyweight material, as lighter fabrics will be too flimsy to hang well. Conversely, light- to medium-weight fabrics make better blinds, as heavy fabrics are often too bulky to fold neatly. Other factors to take into account are the period of the room, which could be highlighted with a fabric of that era, and its size – small rooms are easily overpowered by large-patterned fabrics.

Lastly, bear in mind that curtain fabrics do not have to be purpose-made. As long as you take adequate precautions vis-à-vis fire retardancy, dressmaking fabrics such as sari lengths and suiting cloth, or recycled furnishings such as linen sheets may be cheaper, and more interesting, alternatives.

opposite, above left Utilitarian ticking offers a cheery, cheap and practically indestructible choice, whether you track down densely woven period examples – which are salvaged from old mattresses – or use one of the many modern reinterpretations.

opposite, above right Recycling antique bed and table linen into curtain fabric allows you to make a feature of its wonderful soft drape and eggshell sheen, the result of many years of careful laundering.

opposite, below left Even simple, coarse-weave fabrics make undeniably glamorous curtains when teamed with sumptuous velvet ribbons and a shiny silk lining.

opposite, below right Dressmaking materials like these Indian sari lengths can make inspiring fabric choices, with unusual features like embroidered hems rethought to create decorative leading edges.

this page Fabrics needn't be brightly coloured and ornately patterned to be eye-catching: this fine, self-coloured paisley print needs little more than a delicate beaded trim to finish it off.

plain colours
and weaves

Attaching the adjective 'plain' to anything can suggest a criticism, with the synonyms 'dull' and 'boring' (and the implied accusation of a sartorial cop-out) never far away. But plain/solid fabrics are anything but boring. Think of a swathe of brightly coloured silk and how light plays across its folds, or of a time-worn expanse of rough linen and the charming irregularity of its weave. Both have a character and individuality that are far from dull.

Indeed, the dyes used, the way a plain-coloured yarn is woven, and the treatments applied to the finished fabric, can create amazing variations of subtle pattern. Herringbone, seersucker, bouclé, moiré and chintz are just a few of the disparate 'plains'.

Select a plain fabric in the same way you would choose a paint colour for the walls. If you want the effect to be advancing and dominating, choose a bold colour that contrasts with the rest of the room scheme. For a softer, receding effect, ideal to enhance the sense of space in a small or dark room, choose a pale shade that matches or tones with the other elements.

Where the window dressings will be a prominent and potentially dominant feature in a room (more than likely requiring lots of

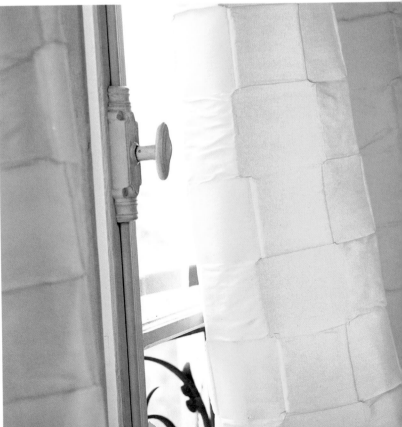

opposite, above right Here a voile curtain in subtle contrasting bands of soft cream is anchored with a border of heavier silk with woven stripes.

opposite, below left This ivory silk satin positively shimmers in the light, bringing texture and interest to its heavy folds.

opposite, below right A bright yellow curtain is far from dull, and the acid tones of the fabric are softened by the embossed interwoven pattern.

this page Plain fabrics make effective layered window treatments. Here floaty voile curtains with a matching pelmet/valance are teamed with a cotton roller blind to provide varying degrees of privacy. The torchon lace edging adds to the feminine effect.

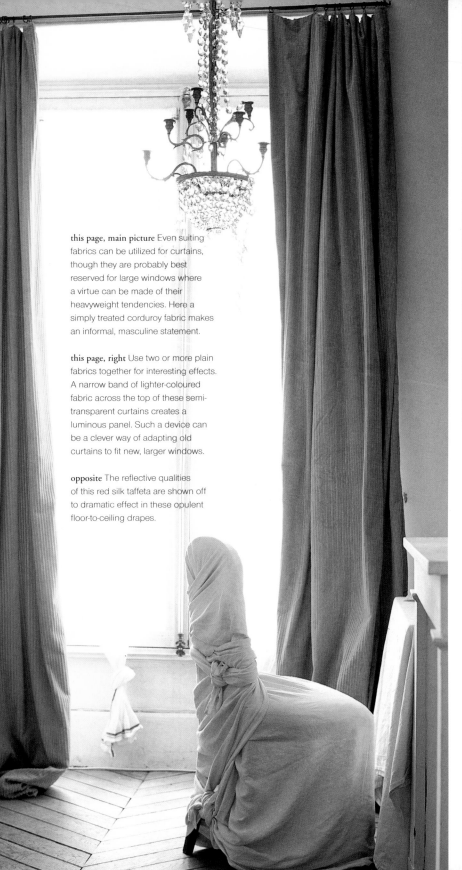

this page, main picture Even suiting fabrics can be utilized for curtains, though they are probably best reserved for large windows where a virtue can be made of their heavyweight tendencies. Here a simply treated corduroy fabric makes an informal, masculine statement.

this page, right Use two or more plain fabrics together for interesting effects. A narrow band of lighter-coloured fabric across the top of these semi-transparent curtains creates a luminous panel. Such a device can be a clever way of adapting old curtains to fit new, larger windows.

opposite The reflective qualities of this red silk taffeta are shown off to dramatic effect in these opulent floor-to-ceiling drapes.

left Teaming two mismatched checks can work well if the colour match is spot-on. Narrow red braiding stitched over the seams stops the confluence of the patterns from looking messy.

above The striped curtains and plaid blanket make natural partners, united by their predominant colour.

opposite, left Edging the hem of this pelmet/valance adds definition, so that the feature does not get lost in the bold pattern.

opposite, centre Ticking is available in multicoloured versions that are perfect for tailored Roman blinds.

opposite, right A courageous pairing of a plaid and check works because the yellows are a perfect match.

geometric patterns

Whether woven or printed, stripes and checks are the most prolific of geometric patterns, coming as they do in almost every combination of colour and scale. Their applications are endless; indeed you only have to contrast the humble ticking with a smart Regency stripe, or a fresh-faced gingham with a bold chequerboard to get an idea of their versatility. Used together, in coordinating proportions and colours, stripes and checks have a natural affinity that makes them a designer favourite – but introduce textural variations into the room if you don't want the results to look too formulaic.

Small checks can bring structure and order to an otherwise busy scheme and team particularly well with toile de Jouy and floral patterns, but stick to coordinating colours. As in fashion,

though perhaps with more flattering results, stripes can be used to mislead the eye. So horizontal stripes can disguise an overly narrow window by creating the illusion of width, while vertical stripes can be used to correct an over-wide window.

Besides stripes and checks, and the cheeriest of geometrics – spots – other options are as varied as the windows that need dressing. When using a multicoloured geometric, such as a plaid, team it with plain fabrics in the predominant colour, or, if you want to go for saturation, more of the same, but think very carefully before introducing other patterns into the mix. Use fashion-led abstract geometrics with caution as they can be easily dated – which is good if you love a particular era but can be bad if that style passes out of favour. And, if you are making the window treatments yourself, be extra careful with geometrics, as any mismatched seams or wonky hems will be more obvious than with a plain or abstract-patterned fabric.

this page Combining pictorial fabrics can be very successful when, as in this Arabian-style canopied room, their colours match exactly and rely on coordinating motifs.

opposite, above A bobble fringe along the leading edge and hem of these toile de Jouy drapes gives structure to the large scale and relative randomness of the pattern. Using red instead of the more obvious navy blue for the trim adds a frivolous touch.

opposite, below left The large floral sprigs on this printed voile are prettily highlighted by the light from the window.

opposite, below centre Small checks in a matching colourway sit easily with this floral and stripe print, while a contrast edging in the dominant colour draws attention to the unusual scalloped pelmet/valance.

opposite, below right Leaving this floral sheer lightly gathered allows the design to be fully appreciated.

florals
and pictorials

From blousey chintzes to history-invoking toile de Jouys, from elegant paisleys to winsome nursery prints, florals and pictorials have the capacity to be both completely charming and completely overwhelming.

If you're using a large-patterned fabric then you're necessarily going to be making a big statement. Can the window and room handle the design? Will you be able to see enough of the pattern to do it justice? Will you (or in the case of nursery prints, your children) still love the design in a few years' time? As with multicoloured geometrics, these fabrics will not easily share room space with other patterns and are best teamed with plain fabrics, small checks or narrow stripes. Unless that is, you make your selection from one of the fabric ranges offering coordinating florals or pictorials. Relying on both a colour and motif theme to unite them, these pairings are best used in unequal proportions to allow one design to dominate. Large-scale patterns will also benefit greatly from grounding with plain edgings or trimmings that pick up the main colour.

By contrast, smaller-scale patterns take on an unobtrusive regularity with the true nature of their design being lost when they are used en masse or seen from a distance, as they would be in a larger room. To do justice to the intricacy of these designs, confine them to more diminutive windows and smaller rooms.

this page By using minimalist hoops and clips on this panel of traditional-style printed velvet, the luxurious look easily adapts to a modern setting.

opposite, above left Expensive fabrics needn't be used en masse to steal the show. Here a floral brocade, used as a border, transforms this ribbed blind.

opposite, above centre Heavyweight fabrics like velvet aren't ideal for blinds, unless, as here, the windows are large enough to give the fabric room to pleat neatly.

opposite, above right A London blind makes a flamboyant window treatment when featuring a beautiful damask. The modest quantity of fabric this style of blind requires makes this a relatively inexpensive way to use a luxurious fabric. Note how the narrow edging defines the characteristic outline of the blind.

opposite, below Theatrical and sumptuous, these peachy velvet curtains with heavy fringed swags make a dramatic focal point in this understated room scheme.

wools, velvets and damasks

Resolutely at the luxurious end of the fabric spectrum, not least because of their cost, wools, velvets and damasks add instant glamour, warmth and a sense of tradition to a room. As such, they are best employed where comfort and smartness are required – living rooms, hallways and bedrooms being the most obvious contenders. The weight of these fabrics (and their consequent drapeability) means that, budget allowing, they will make beautiful, heavily gathered, full-length curtains. To play on their opulent nature, add extravagant trimmings and tiebacks and ornate poles to create a really sumptuous, theatrical effect.

While these fabrics are expensive, they can reasonably be considered a good investment as they will never go out of date. That said, they needn't look entirely traditional or be reserved solely for period interiors. Modern reinterpretations of wool fabrics, for instance, have led to vintage blankets being transformed into 'instant' curtains. Meanwhile, tweeds and suiting fabrics can be used to add a witty, tailored look to a masculine room. Both would look equally at home in an urban loft or a country vicarage.

On a practical note, all curtains made from these heavier fabrics should be lined to give body and to protect them from the ravages of sunlight, which can both fade and destroy natural fibres. Interlining (a third layer sandwiched between the main fabric and lining) will improve the drape of large, traditional curtains, while effectively keeping any draughts at bay.

sheer fabrics

No longer banished to a secondary role hiding behind heavier-weight curtains, sheers have been embraced for their simplicity and ethereal appearance and are, more likely than not, used alone in today's centrally heated and double-glazed homes. In consequence, there has never been a greater choice of natural sheer fabrics available, in both plain and decorative styles.

The cheapest of these is plain cotton muslin/voile, which creates a very soft, simple effect and is ideal for working rooms like kitchens and bathrooms, where curtains need frequent laundering. Other sheer fabrics include the more showy silk organzas and voiles, with their beautiful sheen, and the delicate laces which, removed from their traditional fusty settings, can look surprisingly fresh and pretty. However, with generous natural light, any lightweight, loosely woven fabric will take on a degree of transparency.

The range of decorative sheers is increasing all the time. Embellishments include appliquéd shapes, beads, sequins, tiny mirrors and embroidery, as well as cut-out and devoré work. It is also easy to add embellishment to plain sheers yourself should you decide they need livening-up. Other options include the many sheer fabrics designed for dressmaking – while they may not be sufficiently tough to withstand constant handling or the long-term effects of sunlight that window treatments are subjected to, it may be reasonable to take the view that they don't actually need to last forever.

Coloured sheers can look amazing, although it is worth trying out a sample of fabric at the window before committing yourself, as the effect achieved can alter dramatically depending on the quality of light behind them, and can also radically affect the carefully considered colour scheme of your room. As an inexpensive try-out, consider giving any old sheers, which are looking less than pristine, a new lease of life with a machine dye.

The new generation of double-width fabrics – available in widths of up to 3 metres – is ideal for making sheer curtains. Used sideways with their width as the drop, they mean very large curtains can be made without the need for seams, which not only saves work but looks better, too. These are a particular boon given the current craze for living in open-plan, industrial-type spaces where over-scale curtains and dividers, particularly sheer ones that preserve the architecture and sense of space, come into their own.

opposite, left A variety of semi-transparent materials – including a loosely woven linen stripe and a white-on-white printed voile – shade this sunny corridor in a showcase of the different effects that can be achieved with lightweight fabrics.

opposite, centre Such is the current craze for sheers that even traditional fabrics like toile de Jouy have been reincarnated in voile form. A bobble fringe along the leading edge adds weight and definition.

opposite, right Any loosely woven fabric can be used as a sheer in front of a well-lit window. Here the rough texture of lightweight linen creates a soft, hazy effect.

this page Lace curtains have long been unfairly tarnished by their association with staid, Victorian interiors and ugly nylon nets. Here flat panels of traditional cotton lace look resolutely elegant and feminine.

WORKING WITH PROPORTIONS

Few homeowners are blessed with beautifully proportioned floor-to-ceiling early 19th-century sashes or groovy 1930s Modernist metal windows – at least, not at the moment they become the height of desirability.

Most of us inherit the sort of ill-thought-out features that result from short-sighted cost-cutting, poor design and decades of inappropriate renovations. If this weren't bad enough, tiresome practicalities, such as the need to site radiators on outside walls, have conspired to make matters worse.

Consequently, when devising window treatments, it's often a case of cursing the architect, builder or do-it-yourselfer who created the too small, too narrow or lopsided window you actually have and making the best of a bad job. With a keen eye, it's amazing what visual tricks can be pulled to rectify the imperfect shape or proportion of a window or even the awkward way it is set within the wall. Often these ruses will require a degree of interpretation as no two situations will be quite the same.

Draw your window to scale on graph paper and sketch in your ideas for curtains or a blind to gauge how the approach works in principle. Bear in mind that the window treatment will look quite different when the curtains are closed or the blind is unrolled.

opposite, above left Leaving the wall behind the radiator unpapered and using a fabric that matches the paint colour adds length to this window.

opposite, above right Lightweight shutters that sit within the window frame preserve the architectural proportions of an attractive window.

opposite, below left At first glance, these two windows appear to match, but the one on the left is actually gently curved. The clever use of three Roman blinds maintains the horizontal symmetry and disguises the differences.

opposite, below right Café curtains are the answer to many awkward window shapes. They should align with the central glazing bar for best results.

this page Modern blinds are amazingly flexible and, taking up very little space when retracted, are especially useful in situations with no 'housing' for curtains at the side of the window.

wide windows

Wide windows aren't necessarily a problem – they look wonderful in an Art Deco apartment block, for instance, where they should be emphasized to the full. However, as the Georgian/Federal architects (and the classical scholars who inspired them) knew, the eye is best pleased where the proportions of the feature or building seen replicate ideal geometric shapes such as the square, circle, cube or cube-and-a-half. The greater the deviation from this ideal, the less attractive the feature appears.

Happily, there are ways to restore this balance. Over-wide windows can be visually divided by using several pairs of curtains so one large window is depicted as several smaller ones. This approach can work particularly well where the window stretches the full width of the wall, leaving little room to accommodate the bulk of wide curtains when they are drawn back. It has the disadvantage of significantly reducing the amount of light the room enjoys, which may be a sacrifice worth making if the light in the room is too bright, but to reduce the loss and minimize bulk, use a lightly gathered, light- to medium-weight fabric or opt for a series of blinds instead (from a practical point of view, it would be impossible to make a single blind to span a large area).

Where there is space above the top of the window, another way to disguise excessive width is to exaggerate the apparent height of the window by raising the

Here an inappropriate modern window in a period house has been cunningly disguised with the use of an elaborate pelmet/valance fitted to look as if it is part of the architecture. Allowing the extra-long curtains to overlap the window narrows the width, helping to disguise the shape further. A semi-translucent blind allows light in while blotting out the ugly carpentry.

track or pole to just below the ceiling and hanging floor-length – or even longer – curtains. Any unsightly void could be covered by a pelmet/valance.

Partnering curtains with sheers or blinds to create a layered effect will also obscure the unrelenting horizontal character of a wide window. And, of course, a fabric patterned with vertical stripes – even a subtle self-stripe would do the trick – is a classic disguise for wide windows. The wider the window is, the wider the stripes should be, but you needn't restrict your choice to ready-made striped fabrics. Have fun mixing and matching bands of different fabrics to create an individual design (which can also be a good way of using up remnants), varying the widths of the panels to make the effect easier on the eye. The execution will need to be spot-on, especially where flat panels or blinds are being used as they will offer up any wonky seams for immediate scrutiny. Use ribbons and braids over seams to hide any minor imperfections in the stitching and to accentuate the vertical bands. Another variation on this theme would be to use loose contrasting lengths of ribbon or braid as long, decorative ties for curtain headings or as hold-ups for unstructured pleated and rolled Swedish blinds. These will, again, help visually to chop up the width.

below far left A blind made from two toning silk fabrics (both of which are also used in the matching padded pelmet/valance) shows that with careful measuring and making up a 'homemade' stripe can create a dramatic effect. Here the decorative trimming serves to hide the seams and to highlight the vertical bands.

below centre Floor-to-ceiling drapes in a subtle self-stripe fabric soften the dominating effect of these vast picture windows in a city skyscraper by reducing the apparent width. The curtain track is mounted on the ceiling to make use of every inch of available height.

below right Something as simple as using a contrasting colour for the ties in these pleated blinds adds vertical demarcation and breaks up the width of these wide, shallow windows. As these blinds are designed to be left partially unfurled to obscure the view, they mask some of the available light, so they are left unlined and made with a lightweight, loosely woven fabric.

above This trio of blinds has been tailored to match the window architecture and allow the side windows to be open whilst still maintaining privacy in the bathroom.

far left Although a single curtain rail has been fitted across this run of recessed sashes, individual sill-length curtains in a transparent material allow the window architecture to predominate.

left This wide window in an Art Deco apartment suits the scale of the room and is enhanced and celebrated by the horizontal 'skeleton' of a semi-transparent Roman blind.

no-sew sheet curtains

Antique linen has a unique quality that only comes after years of use and laundering. Monogrammed sheets, hand towels and lace-edged tablecloths can be sourced from textile auctions, specialist shops or flea markets. They can then easily be adapted as curtains and, if decorative clips are used to fix them onto a metal rod or wire, require no sewing.

MATERIALS AND EQUIPMENT
sheet
tailor's chalk
curtain clips

MEASURING UP
The pelmet/valance should be between ⅛ and ¼ the height of the window, but the exact depth will depend on the size of the cloth and the shape of the window.

VARIATION
Embroidered hand towels (left) have been made into half-curtains with simple clips. Sunlight filters through the eyelet work to give a warm translucency to the starched linen.

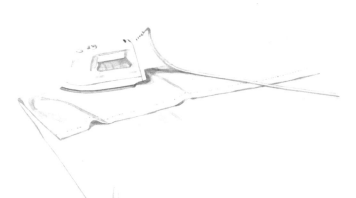

1 Wash the sheet at a high temperature to remove any marks or crease lines and iron well to restore its original appearance. Turn the top edge forwards to form a pelmet/valance and press along the fold.

2 Using tailor's chalk, mark a point at each top corner. Draw a series of equally spaced points between them, one for each curtain clip.

3 Fix the clips in place and hang the curtain from the pole.

opposite These narrow, floor-length windows have been given extra width by extending the curtain pole well beyond the architrave. Keeping the heading of ornate curtains stationery – and holding them back with extra-long tiebacks – helps to disguise the visual trickery.

this page These recessed French windows have been treated like bay windows. A three-sided curtain rail/rod not only makes the feature appear much wider and more in proportion than it really is, but enables curtains to be positioned well out of harm's way when the doors are in use.

tall windows

When dealing with tall, narrow windows, you need simply to reverse the approach taken for wide windows. Sill-length curtains are often the best choice. They will help by effectively truncating the perceived length of the window, whereas floor-length drapes will necessarily draw attention to the vertical height.

Where floor-length curtains are required, you can increase the apparent width of the window by extending the pole or track well beyond the edges of the frame. This will create the illusion of a much wider feature and can be especially effective where the tall window is marooned in a large expanse of wall. If you do take this option, be mindful that when the curtains are drawn back, they will need to have enough body to comfortably fill this extra housing or wall space.

If you can afford to cut down on the available light in the room, another trick would be to reduce the apparent height of the window by setting a deep pelmet/valance as close to the top of the window frame as possible, since this will have the effect of bisecting the window.

The classic cosmetic disguise is to employ horizontal bands, either in the form of a striped fabric or a curtain or blind made up of several different horizontal panels. Also consider attaching a deep border in a contrasting colour to plain/solid-coloured floor-length curtains (roughly one-third of the height of the overall curtain in depth) which will draw the eye down, making the curtain appear shorter than it is. Similarly, an integral

below Here a plain metal curtain pole has been suspended from a ceiling beam which, together with the extra-long curtains spilling onto the floor, creates the illusion that this truncated narrow window is really a more attractive floor-to-ceiling version.

right Used with restraint, an ornamental heading will subtly draw attention. The tasselled pennants that bisect the top of these plain curtains draw the eye above the top of the

frame to the classical, reeded pole. The pole itself extends beyond the width of the window to add importance to this modestly sized living-room window.

far right The large-scale checks of this woven fabric echo the grid created by the heavy glazing bars of a balconied window overlooking a city square. The curtains have been left unlined to maximize the amount of light that enters the room.

pelment/valance (again, roughly one-third of the height of the overall curtain in depth) in a contrasting, lighter colour will break up the vertical length.

A simple sill-length café curtain that neatly bisects the window or a blind constructed from a carefully chosen fabric – again the obvious being a horizontal stripe or several different horizontal panels – eradicate the awkwardness of tall windows that stop short of the floor, an aspect that floor-length curtains would tend to draw attention to. Blinds are particularly useful for tall windows where the architrave extends right up to the ceiling, preventing a pole or track being fitted to the outside of the frame.

tie-top bordered curtain

Natural cotton, which hangs in soft folds, lends itself to this informal tied heading. The curtain is folded into a series of deep pleats without any reinforcement and is given extra weight by the deep border of unbleached linen. The seam is embellished with a row of herringbone stitch. If you are making the curtain from a lighter fabric or to cover a smaller window than that shown here, you should reduce the size of the pleats accordingly.

MATERIALS AND EQUIPMENT
unbleached linen
cream cotton fabric
matching sewing thread
small safety pin
cream embroidery thread
basic sewing kit

MEASURING UP
A = length of curtain pole
B = from bottom of curtain rings to floor

TO CALCULATE THE NUMBER OF PLEATS
The pleats are at 10cm (4in) intervals and each one takes up 20cm (8in) of fabric. Divide A by 10 and subtract 1 to find out the number required.

CUTTING OUT
main curtain:
width = number of pleats x 30cm (12in) plus 6cm (2in)
length = ¾ B plus 6cm (2in)

border:
width = number of pleats x 30cm (12in) plus 6cm (2in)
length = ¼ B plus 6cm (2in)

ties:
Cut one for each pleat
width = 6cm (2in)
length = 30cm (12cm)

1 Pin and tack/baste the border to the bottom of the main curtain. Machine stitch 1.5cm (½in) from the edge and press the seam open.

2 Press under a 1.5 cm (½in) double hem along each side of the curtain. Pin and tack/baste, then machine stitch.

3 Press under 1.5cm (½in) along the top, then press under another 3cm (1in). Pin, tack/baste and machine stitch. Turn up the hem in the same way, finishing off by hand if preferred (see Practicalities, page137).

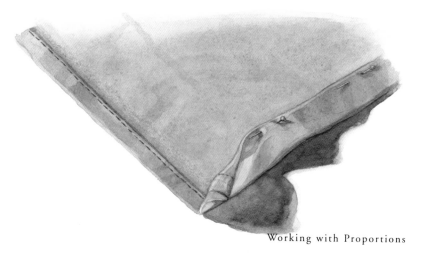

4 To make each tie, fold a strip in half lengthways. Pin and tack/baste the long edges together and machine stitch leaving a 5mm (¼in) seam allowance. Fasten a safety pin to one open end. Feed the pin back through the fabric tube to turn it the right way out. Unpin, then press flat so that the seam lies along one side. Turn under 5mm (¼in) to neaten the raw edges and close with slip stitch.

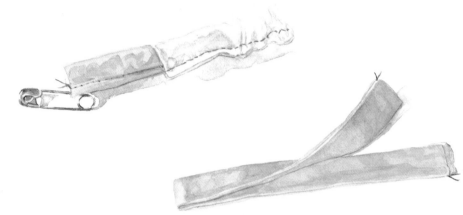

5 To mark the positions of the pleats: insert a pin 15cm (6in) from each corner of the top edge; place a row of pins at approximately 30cm (12in) intervals; mark a point 10cm (4in) either side of each pin using tailor's chalk.

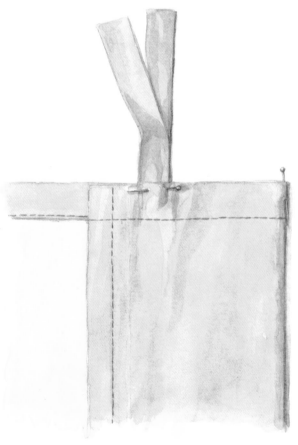

6 Starting at the left corner and working from the right side of the fabric, pin and tack/baste 1.5cm (⅝in) of the folded end of a tie between the first and second chalk marks. Remove the marker pin which now lies at the centre front of the pleat.

7 Attach the other ties, fixing each one between two chalk marks, leaving 10cm (4in) of fabric between each pleat. Machine stitch across the bottom of the ties, 5mm (¼in) from the top of the curtain. Work a few reverse stitches at each end to strengthen the row.

8 Finish off by working a row of herringbone stitch (see Practicalities, page 137) over the join between the curtain and the border.

9 Knot each tie securely to a curtain ring in order to hang the curtain.

top row, left Unlined tab-top curtains provide a simple treatment and, being insubstantial, leave the window relatively unobscured when open.

top row, centre These tightly gathered lightweight cotton curtains are full enough to be decorative and not too skimpy, yet not so heavy as to obscure the window.

top row, right The pole for these floor-to-eave curtains is ingeniously suspended between two rafters.

bottom row, left A tray cloth makes an easy café curtain at this diminutive sash and offers privacy during the day.

bottom row, centre Most large-scale patterns are wasted over a small area, except that is for airy, random designs like this embroidered sheer.

bottom row, right To make the curtains floor or sill length is a dilemma with small windows. This solution, twisting the bulk of the fabric over a holdback, is good compromise.

small windows

With small windows, where insulation is unlikely to be too much of a problem, it may be that you can do without curtains or blinds altogether and merely enjoy the porthole-like glimpses of the outside world. Where a window treatment is necessary, any loss of light will be keenly felt, so a design that does not obscure the glass will be required.

All the techniques for disguising wide or tall windows can be applied to small windows, although they will have to be adapted to suit the more diminutive proportions. So, for example, use pinstripes rather than ordinary stripes, horizontally or vertically, to broaden or narrow as required. Avoid large-scale patterned fabrics altogether, except for a medium-sized window, where an airy, abstract design can help to disguise a boxy shape.

Whether floor-length curtains will work depends largely on how high or low the window is positioned in the wall – too far either way and they will look ridiculous.

Where there is little room to draw back the curtains, use only very lightweight fabrics that will gather and hang comfortably in a confined space. Consider, too, reducing the amount of fabric used by applying a smaller ratio of fabric widths than normal or by cutting back to a simple panel. Low-key headings, such as ties or curtain clips, will probably work best in these instances.

For recessed attic or dormer windows, where a normal treatment would obscure the light, sill-length curtains hung from portière rods that open out like shutters offer a nifty solution. For

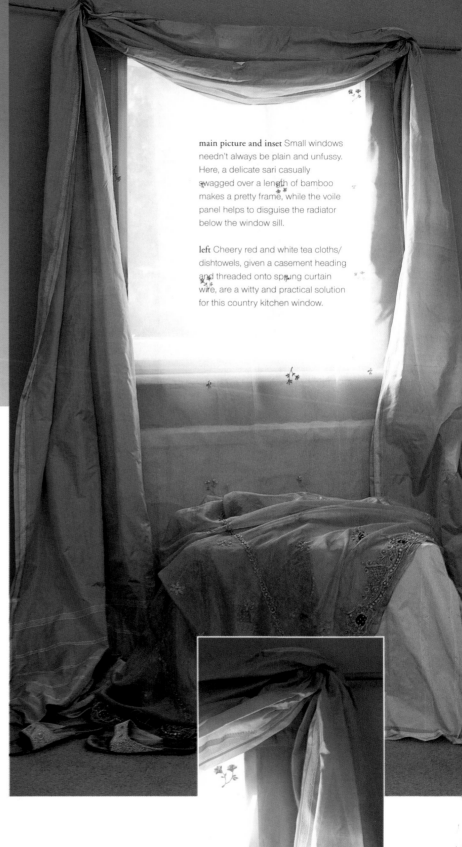

main picture and inset Small windows needn't always be plain and unfussy. Here, a delicate sari casually swagged over a length of bamboo makes a pretty frame, while the voile panel helps to disguise the radiator below the window sill.

left Cheery red and white tea cloths/ dishtowels, given a casement heading and threaded onto sprung curtain wire, are a witty and practical solution for this country kitchen window.

a more tailored, minimal look, use roller or Swedish blinds, which take up less space when retracted than Roman or (heaven forbid!) Austrian/balloon blinds, or hang the latter styles outside the window frame or recess to minimize the loss of light.

Where privacy is required or an unattractive view needs to be hidden, consider whether a sheer might not be sufficient alone, as a layered treatment could look fussy and heavy. For an even cleaner solution, a half sheer hung at the same height as the central glazing bar might preserve modesty and satisfy aesthetic ideals while still allowing plenty of precious light into the room.

One way in which small windows surpass all others is in their modest fabric requirements. They offer the perfect opportunity to use up left-over fabrics or, less frugally, to select the most desirable fabrics that would be too expensive for larger projects. They also make the perfect recipient for carefully hoarded pieces of antique bed and table linen, which are sadly rarely used today for their original purpose.

double-sided dormer curtain

A hinged portière rod that swings out to lie flat against the adjacent wall during the day is the ideal solution for a small dormer window. Both the front and back of the curtain will be visible at different times, so they should be equally attractive. This reversible panel is made from a plain fabric with a woven border, backed and piped with coordinating gingham. The method can be simplified by leaving out the piping/cording (skip steps 1–3).

MATERIALS AND EQUIPMENT
main fabric
backing fabric
fine piping cord
matching sewing thread
long ruler/yardstick
portière rod to fit width of window frame
drill, screwdriver and screws
basic sewing kit

MEASURING UP
A = length of portière rod
B = from 4cm (1½in) above top of portière rod to sill

CUTTING OUT
front and back alike
width = A plus 10cm (4in) for seams and fullness
length = B plus 4cm (1½in) for seams

PIPING CORD
length = 2A + 2B plus 30cm (12in)

1 Cut a 5cm (2in) wide strip of gingham to cover the piping cord. Join pieces as necessary to reach the required length and press the seams open. Fold the strip over the cord with the right side outwards and pin, then tack/baste in place close to the cord.

2 Starting 5–10cm (2–4in) from one top corner and leaving a 4 cm (1½in) loose end, pin the piping/cording around the right side of the front panel, matching the raw edges. Clip into the seam allowance at the corners. Tack/baste down, leaving a 4cm (1½in) overlap.

3 Take out the tacking/basting for 4cm (1½in) at each end of the piping/cording. Trim the cord so the two ends butt up and stitch them together loosely. Press a 1cm (½in) turning at the end of one strip. Fold it over the other strip and tack/baste through all the layers. Fit a zip foot to the machine and stitch down 3 mm (⅛in) from the cord all around the panel.

4 With right sides together, pin and tack/baste the front and back panels together. If you are using piping, it will be sandwiched between the two pieces of fabric (as shown, right).

5 With the reverse side of the front panel facing upwards, mark two points on each side 3cm (1¼in) and 8cm (3in) down from the top corners. Leave the spaces between these marks unstitched to form the openings for the casing.

6 Machine stitch around the seams 1cm (½in) from outside edge, working a few extra stitches to reinforce the beginning and end of each row. (If you have included the piping/cording, you will need to use a zip foot and should stitch as close to the cord as possible.) Leave a 20cm (8in) gap along the centre of the top edge for turning right side out.

7 Clip the surplus fabric from the corners and turn the curtain right sides out through the top opening. Ease the corners into shape using a large knitting needle or similar blunt point. Finish off the top edge by pressing under the unstitched seam allowance, then pin, tack/baste and slip stitch it down.

8 Using a dressmaker's pen and a long ruler/yardstick, draw two lines between the top and bottom of the side openings to mark the casing. Tack/baste, then machine stitch along these lines. Press the curtain.

9 Screw the bracket to the top of the window and slot the portière arm in position. Slide the casing over the arm to hang the curtain.

patchwork panel

Collect fragments of antique fabrics to make this patchwork kitchen curtain. Delicate white cottons – embroidered lawn, drawn-thread work and broderie anglaise/eyelet lace – work especially well against a window. The panel is edged with lace and hung from a narrow white rod with a row of checked ribbon loops. This project is very individual and can be adapted to suit whatever interesting pieces of fabric and edgings you can find – the result will be unique.

MATERIALS AND EQUIPMENT
embroidered fabric
gingham
check ribbon
cotton lace
matching sewing thread
basic sewing kit

MEASURING UP
width = length of curtain rod plus 10cm (4in) for fullness
length = from 5cm (2in) below pole to 5cm (2in) above sill

1 Wash and press all the fabric. Cut out a selection of strips and rectangles, discarding any worn areas.

2 Lay the fabric pieces out, taking time to create a balanced arrangement. Add an extra 1.5cm (½in) around each piece for seaming when calculating the required width and length.

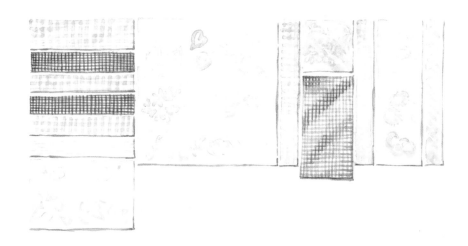

3 Join all the horizontal seams first, using a narrow French seam. With wrong sides together, pin and tack/baste two pieces together. Machine stitch 7mm (¼in) from the edge. Trim the seam allowance to 3mm (⅛in) and refold so that the right sides are together. Stitch again, 7mm (¼in) from the fold. Press the seam to one side.

4 Join the vertical seams in the same way, then trim the sides of the panel, if necessary, so that they are straight.

5 Press under 1.5cm (½in) around all four sides. Fold the edges up to the crease and press again to make a narrow double hem. Tack/baste and machine stitch down.

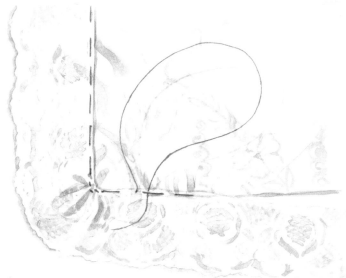

6 Tack/baste a length of lace around the panel, gathering it slightly as you go to fit around the corners. Slip stitch the two ends together, then machine stitch close to the edge.

7 The loops are made from 12cm (5in) lengths of ribbon. Press under 1.5cm (½in) at each end and slip stitch together along the folds. Pin along the wrong side of the top edge at intervals of approximately 15cm (6in). Slip stitch in place and hang from the rod.

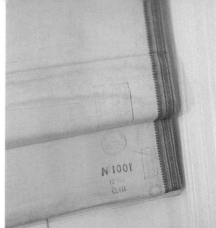

bays, recesses and awkward shapes

Ironically it is often the most interesting windows that are the most difficult to devise window treatments for, with arched and round windows being obvious examples. Indeed, their very attractiveness begs the question: is it really necessary to disguise them with curtains or blinds? But where this can't be avoided, there are several ways in which their merits can be preserved, the most obvious solution being to extend the track well beyond the architrave or recess so the curtain can be pulled well clear. The disadvantage with this is that the window is hidden completely when the curtains are closed.

The graceful sweep of an arched window, in particular, can be maintained and further emphasized by using curtains with a fixed heading that replicates the curve by means of a flexible track. These have the disadvantage of reducing the light coming into the room and, perhaps, look a little fussy in today's pared-down interiors. A more minimal solution would be to use a half, café-style curtain to screen the lower portion of the window while leaving the

opposite Here, individual roller blinds, in an unobtrusive plain white fabric that blends with the paintwork, provide any necessary screening without detracting from the leaded windows or the owner's unusual decorative flourishes.

this page A vintage bolt of fabric featuring an attractive braided border has been ingeniously used to make coordinated Roman blinds at a bay window. To have used curtains in this situation – with such a beautiful architrave and cornice – would have been sacrilege. At the opposite end of the same room, a similar fabric has been chosen for curtains.

glorious arch unimpaired. A roller blind fixed to the sill and extended upwards would discretely achieve the same result.

With bay and bow windows, there are two main options: either to hang the window treatment along the window shape or outside the recess. If privacy is not an issue, the latter is by far the easiest, less light-stealing solution, although you will be effectively sacrificing any usable floor area, or sill display space in the case of bow windows, when the curtains are closed.

Where you want to follow the shape of the window, the available options will be dictated by the window itself. Both a bow-shaped window and a three-sided bay can be fitted with a flexible curtain track or a single pole, though the latter will have to be specially made. Alternatively, they can be treated as a series of smaller windows and given individual blinds or curtains – lightly gathered to minimize loss of light – hung from separate poles or tracks. What can work well is to combine both approaches, with sheers or blinds against the windows and full-length, possibly false curtains hung outside the window recess, perhaps with a swag across the top to create a theatrical frame.

opposite These three solutions to the challenges of dressing a bay window are equally successful. A quirky custom-made wrought-iron rail provides an interesting focal point, while café curtains or more formal London blinds suspended within the individual frames obviate the need for specially made poles and show off the windows' architecture to the full.

above The horizontal struts in these six blinds dramatically enhance the geometrical feel of this window.

left By recognizing that the blinds in this sun room need to do very different jobs – screening the view on one side and filtering the sun on the other – a solution was found for these awkwardly shaped windows.

Working with Proportions   51

London blind

The arrangement of this blind has been designed to allow for the security gates on the window to be opened and closed easily, without hindering the look of the window treatment. Its dramatic billowing curves are mounted outside the window recess at ceiling height from a wooden pelmet board angled at the corners to emphasize the fullness that comes from the deep inverted pleat at either side of the heading.

MATERIALS AND EQUIPMENT

plain/solid fabric with a textured weave

matching sewing thread

large set square/carpenter's square and long ruler/yardstick

Velcro/touch-and-close tape

1.5cm (½in) plastic blind rings

nylon blind cord

blind acorn/blind pull

basic sewing kit

for the board:

3 x 10cm (1½ x 4in) wooden plank, the width
of window frame plus 30cm (12in) overlap

pencil

saw, drill, rawlplugs/plugs and screws

sandpaper

paint to match fabric

staple gun

2 angle brackets

cleat and screws

3 screw-eyes

MAKING THE BOARD

Mark two points on one long edge of the plank 15cm (6in) in from the corners. Draw
a line from each point to the corner below it, then saw along these two lines. Sand
any rough edges and paint the wood to match the fabric. When the paint has dried,
cut a length of Velcro/touch-and-close tape to fit along the front edge of the board.
Separate the two pieces and staple the hooked side in place. Screw an angle
bracket 30cm (12in) from each corner and fix to the wall, centrally above the
window. Put a screw-eye towards the back of the underside 15cm (6in) in from
each corner, and the third 5cm (2in) from the right edge.

MEASURING

A = length of board plus 6cm (2in)

B = from ceiling to 3cm (1¼in) below
bottom edge of frame or sill

CUTTING OUT

width = A plus 60cm (24in) for pleats plus
4cm (2in) for hems

depth = B plus 4cm (2in) for hems

Cut 2 cords to the following lengths:
2B; 2B plus A

1 Press a 1cm (½in) turning along each side of the fabric. Fold over a second time to make a double hem and press. Pin, tack/baste and machine stitch close to the inner fold. Hem the bottom in the same way.

2 Mark the two pleats by cutting three small notches along the top, 18cm (7in), 33cm (13in) and 48cm (19in) in from each corner.

3 On the wrong side of the fabric, draw a chalk line parallel to each side, in line with the centre notch of each pleat. Mark the positions for the rings at 40cm (16in) intervals along each line, starting at the bottom edge.

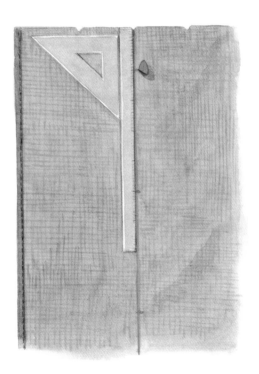

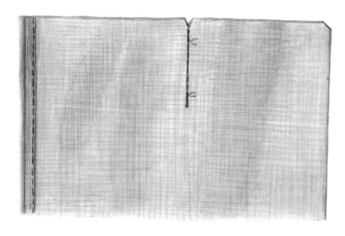

4 With right sides together, fold the blind lengthways so the first and third notches at one corner meet. Draw a 10cm (4in) chalk line on the wrong side at this point and pin along it. Do the same at the other corner and check the position of the pleats against the board. They should lie across the angles; adjust if necessary. Tack/baste and machine down, working extra stitches at each end to secure the row.

5 Match the centre notches to the seams and open out the fabric at each side to make inverted pleats. Pin and tack/baste together through all the layers. Machine stitch 1cm (½in) from the edge and press.

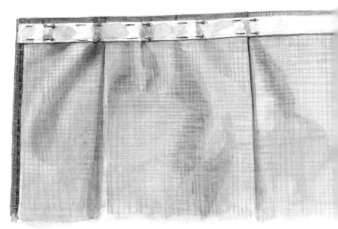

6 Press under a 2cm (1in) turning along the top of the blind. Pin and tack/baste the second length of Velcro/touch-and-close tape to the back, 5mm (¼in) from the fold. Machine stitch, starting each row from the same end of the tape to prevent the fabric puckering.

7 Sew a blind ring to each of the points marked in step 3.

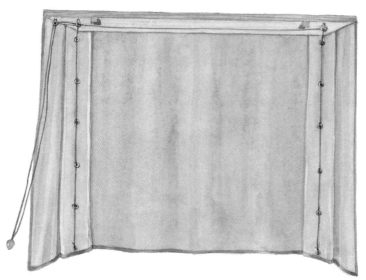

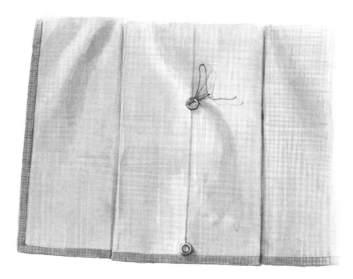

8 Knot the two cords securely to the bottom rings and thread them upwards. Attach the blind to the batten, lining up the two pieces of Velcro/touch-and-close tape carefully. Stand between the blind and the window to complete the stringing. Thread cord on your left (as seen above) through the screw-eye immediately above and then through the eye to the left. Take the other cord through the screw-eye above it, then across through the other two eyes.

9 Fix the cleat to the right side of the window frame. Trim the cords so that they end just below the cleat. Attach the blind acorn/blind pull and knot in place.

VARIATION

This simplified version (right and far right) is suitable when the blind does not need to be built around a recess. It is made from two narrow panels of sheer fabric joined with a French seam (see Practicalities, page 136). It is mounted with Velcro to a narrow strip of wood set within the frame so that it lies flat against the window. The rings are attached to the back of the side hems and centre seam at 25cm (10in) intervals to create two soft curves when the blind is drawn up.

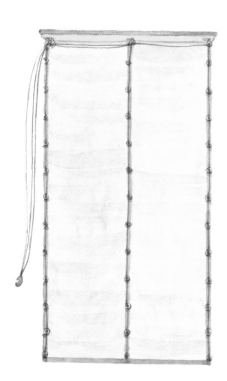

French windows,
doors and cupboards

Most French windows and external glazed doors, whether they lead onto a terrace, balcony or garden, are designed to frame an outside view that should be enjoyed to the full. For this reason, choose a window treatment and a fabric that combine to enhance rather than detract from the vista and allow it to be appreciated at all times. Plain or subtly patterned fabrics are the obvious contenders. As the windows will frequently be open, it is a good idea to select fabrics and treatments that are easily laundered as they will soon become grubby with dust and the constant traffic passing by.

Unlike most other window styles, French windows and glazed doors have the practical requirement that access through them should not be restricted, so fixed headings should be avoided. Likewise, heavily gathered or lined and

opposite A series of disparate glazed doors and windows are unified by eye-catching swagged pelmets/valances in a bold striped fabric.

left Ceiling-mounted rods that keep the curtain away from the window architrave are useful for floor-to-ceiling French windows.

right Firmly tied back, decorative sheer curtains allow easy access through these French windows while softening the dominating expanse of glass.

below At first glance you wouldn't know these understated curtains were there, so well do they blend into the background.

interlined curtains are not ideal, especially where there is not enough housing space for the fabric to hang clear of the doors when the curtains are drawn back. Fixed tiebacks or holdbacks are a useful accessory here, both to keep curtains clear of the opening and to prevent them flapping in the breeze. And even if ease of access is not an overwhelming consideration, because the windows are reasonably wide, for example, bear in mind that any doors that open inwards will inevitably catch on full curtains and eventually damage them in the process.

Where the doors will only be used with any regularity in the summer and the delights of the view are similarly seasonal, consider changing the window treatment in winter, when a heavier, cosier style might be welcome, especially if the doors are at all draughty.

Working with Proportions 57

Many of the disadvantages of wide or tall windows apply to French windows, so adapt the relevant solutions to suit the practicalities of a thoroughfare. For example, where there is more than one pair of French windows in a row, breaking up the expanse of glass with a series of individual curtains would probably be impractical, unless they are lightweight enough to be drawn well clear of the doors in daytime. Several blinds, on the other hand, might work well.

For tall or narrow windows and doors, techniques such as extending the pole or track beyond the window frame to add the appearance of width will have practical as well as visual benefits.

Where blinds or curtains fixed directly to the frame of a glazed door are being considered, remember that if the door opens outwards they will be exposed to the weather.

above Extending the curtain pole well beyond the sides of these arched French doors allows the full, boldly checked curtains, with a gypsy-style gathered hem, to hang clear of the doors during the day. The patterned pelmet/valance draws the eye upwards, diverting attention from what has become a wide-looking window.

right Where the worktops do not allow the curtains to be drawn clear of the doorway, lightly gathered panels in a small, obtrusive check are the order of the day. Simple tie tabs suit the informality of setting and can be easily taken down for cleaning.

MATERIALS AND EQUIPMENT
lightweight to medium-weight fabric
matching sewing thread
heading buckram 10cm (4in) deep
curtain hooks
basic sewing kit

MEASURING UP
A = ½ length of pole
B = from bottom of rings to floor

CALCULATING THE PLEAT ALLOWANCE
The pleats are 12cm (5in) apart with a 6cm (2½in) space at each corner. Divide A by 12cm (5in) to find out how many you will need and round up or down to the nearest whole number. Multiply this figure by 15cm (6in) to find out how much extra fabric is needed to make the pleats.

CUTTING OUT
If necessary join lengths of fabric to the required width using a narrow French seam (see Practicalities, page 136).

width = A plus pleat allowance plus 12cm (5in) for hems plus overlap allowance, if required
length = B plus 11cm (4½in) for heading allowance plus 15cm (6in) for hems

Cut a length of buckram 2cm (1in) shorter than the width of the curtain panel

unlined triple-pleat curtains

Unlined curtains are usually made from a lighter weight of fabric than lined curtains, which allows daylight to filter through. Ready-made tapes designed to create instant pleated headings are easy to use, but it is worth making headings by hand in the traditional way because they give a crisper, more professional finish and can be adapted to create accurate pleats on striped or checked fabrics. Buckram – a coarse cloth stiffened with size – gives rigidity to the headings.

1 For each curtain, turn under and press a 3cm (1¼ in) double hem along each side edge and a 7.5cm (3in) double hem along the bottom edge.

2 Mark three points with pins: the corner, the inside edge of the side turning where it meets the hem, and the corresponding point on the hem.

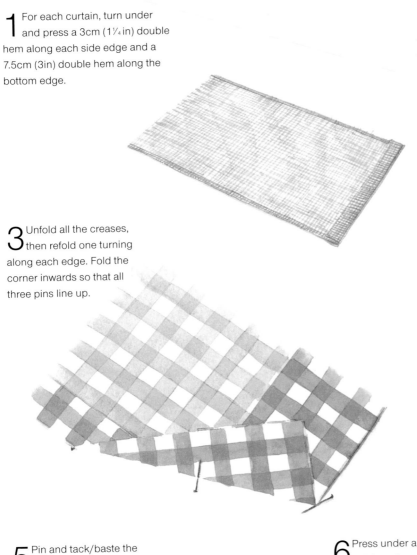

3 Unfold all the creases, then refold one turning along each edge. Fold the corner inwards so that all three pins line up.

4 Press lightly, then refold and pin down the second turnings. Slip stitch the two sides of the mitre together, from the corner inwards.

5 Pin and tack/baste the side and bottom hems. Machine or slip stitch the side hems, and slip or herringbone stitch the bottom hem.

6 Press under a 1cm (½in) turning along the top raw edge. Starting 1cm (½in) in from one corner, pin the top edge of the buckram under the fold. Tack/baste and machine stitch it in place.

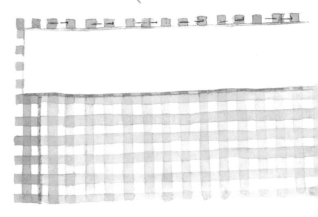

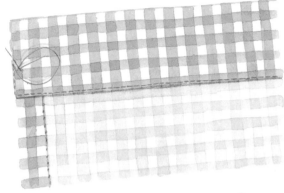

7 Fold the buckram to the wrong side and press along the fold. Slip stitch together the side edges of the fold.

8 Using tailor's chalk, mark the positions of the pleats and the gaps between them along the wrong side of the top edge.

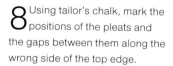

9 Pin two pleat lines together to make a large pleat. Tack/baste and machine stitch on the right side to just below the bottom edge of the buckram.

10 Hand pleat the fabric into three equal-sized small folds, then press them into position. Pin, tack/baste and machine stitch across the folds 1cm (½in) below the bottom edge of the buckram, at right angles to the pleat lines.

11 Sew a curtain hook securely to the top of each pleat, on the wrong side of the heading. If the curtain is to hang from decorative rings on a pole, the top of the hooks should be 1cm (½in) below the top edge of the curtain. If the curtain is to hang from a track, the top of the hooks should be 5cm (2in) down, so that the track is concealed when the curtains are drawn.

this page Curtains make inexpensive screens to open shelving in rooms where clutter and mess need disguising. Here, box-pleated panels in a snazzy metallic fabric are suspended from a plain metal bar using a heavy-duty combination of eyelets and screw clips. The wipe-clean material is ideal for its setting in a working kitchen.

opposite, above This sumptuous living room has been lined with green velvet across its walls, and the same fabric has been chosen to make up the drapes. Lightly gathered with traditional triple pleats and hung from a plain, narrow pole, the curtains make this doorway effectively 'disappear' when drawn.

In some cases it might be more practical to attach a roller blind – which takes up little space when pulled up – to the retaining frame.

For fully or partially glazed internal doors, where privacy or hiding domestic mess are the main concerns rather than light, heat or noise insulation, consider Roman, Swedish or roller blinds. For a softer look, use fixed decorative panels – an antique tea towel/dishtowel or a lacey tray cloth are perfect for this use and have the bonus of being relatively instant options requiring little sewing.

Fixed curtains gathered onto sprung curtain wires or narrow rods at the top and bottom of the window also look neat. Choose a lightweight fabric in a plain/solid or small-patterned geometric fabric, as larger-scale patterns will become lost in the tight gathers. Being attached to the frame at the top and bottom keeps the window treatment firmly anchored on the moving door, but has the disadvantage of making it inflexible, so the window is obscured at all times, which should be borne in mind if light is restricted. The gathered curtain solution works particularly well for glazed or open cupboard doors, introducing a sweet country style in gingham for a kitchen or a more sophisticated look in a sheer fabric for built-in wardrobes/closets in a bedroom.

If the door is recessed in the eaves or is positioned in a corner of the room, you may prefer to use hinged portière rods, which mean that the curtain can be swung back to one side when necessary.

below far left An antique cupboard that is missing its original glazing is given a new lease of life with lightly gathered panels of gingham set behind chicken wire.

below centre left Minimalist white curtains look suitably modern at these floor-to-ceiling French windows while adding a softening and light-filtering touch to a contemporary kitchen.

below The pole for these casement-headed door curtains is held in place with a wing screw, meaning it can be easily disassembled when the curtains need cleaning.

cupboard curtains

A minimal amount of sewing is needed to create these curtains. Each panel is a simple rectangle, hemmed along each side and gathered at the top and bottom. The gingham curtains are drawn up with elastic and pinned in place, while the more formal folds of the plain curtains are created by using sprung curtain wire. Washable, lightweight and sheer cotton furnishing or dressmaking fabrics are most suitable because they hang in fine folds. Small prints, plain colours or geometric stripes and checks work best, as large-scale patterns become lost when gathered.

MATERIALS AND EQUIPMENT
cotton fabric
matching sewing thread
basic sewing kit

for the gingham curtains:
narrow braid elastic
small safety pin
drawing pins/thumbtacks

for the plain curtains:
pencil and bradawl/awl
4 screw-eyes and 4 cup hooks for
each curtain
sprung curtain wire
heavy wire cutters

MEASURING UP AND CUTTING OUT
The finished curtain should overlap the glass or mesh by 3cm (1¼in) at each side.

width = 1½–2 x width of door panel (depending on weight of fabric) plus 6cm (2½in) overlap plus 4cm (1½in) hem allowance

length = depth of panel plus 6cm (2½in) overlap plus 6cm (2½in) for the headings

MAKING THE CURTAINS

1 Iron the fabric to remove any creases. Press under 1cm (½in) along each side edge. Press under another 1cm (½in) to make a double hem, then pin, tack/baste and machine stitch close to the inner fold. If the fabric is not the same on both sides, make the hems on the right side of the curtain.

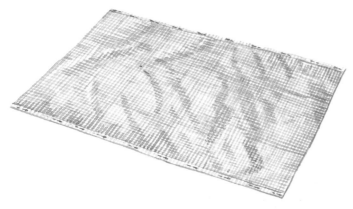

2 Press under 1cm (½in) along the bottom edge, then press under another 2cm (¾in). Pin, tack/baste and machine stitch close to the inner fold to form a narrow channel or cased heading. Do the same at the top edge and finish off any loose threads.

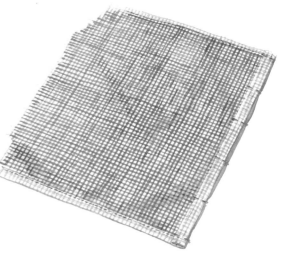

HANGING THE GINGHAM CURTAINS

1 Cut a length of braid elastic 4cm (1½in) shorter than the width of the door panel. Fix a safety pin to one end and pass it along the bottom casing. Draw the elastic through until the loose end is in line with the opening, then stab stitch it securely in place, through the front and back of the casing.

2 Bring the pin out at the other opening and sew the end of the elastic to the casing. Thread the top casing in the same way.

3 With hems and casings facing the door, attach the curtain to the inside of the cupboard using drawing pins/thumbtacks at the top and bottom edges.

HANGING THE PLAIN CURTAINS

1 Mark four points on the back of the cupboard door, 3cm (1¼in) from each corner of the opening. Use a bradawl/awl to make a hole at each mark and screw the cup hooks into the door so that they face upwards.

3 Cut the wire to length and twist the second eye in place. Do the same with the second piece of wire.

4 Feed the two wires into the top and bottom casings; the fabric will gather up as it goes through.

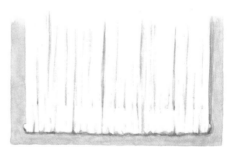

5 Hook the top wire in place so that the hems and casings face the door, then slip the bottom screw-eyes over the hooks.

2 Twist a screw-eye into one end of the sprung wire and loop it over a hook. Stretch the wire across to the second hook – it should be taut but not too tight – and make a pencil mark on the wire where they meet.

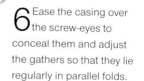

6 Ease the casing over the screw-eyes to conceal them and adjust the gathers so that they lie regularly in parallel folds.

this page Simple linen drapes in a soothing shade of blue enwrap a day bed, to create a cosy, private retreat in an open-plan apartment.

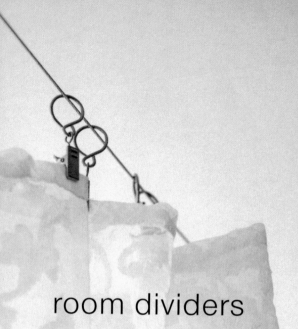

main picture Lightweight fabrics, such as this cotton voile, can be suspended from tension wire to create an unobtrusive divider.

above right A modern take on the beaded curtain: lengths of chrome chain make an unusual screen.

centre right Unusual fabrics, like this dévoré velvet sheer, can elevate a functional screen to a thing of beauty.

below right In a small studio where a room-width divider would restrict space, a mosquito net is a clever way to camouflage the bed from the living room during the day.

room dividers

With the fashion for open-plan living comes the predicament of what to do about privacy and the inevitable mess on view for all the world to see, not to mention the echoes and draughts which big spaces encourage. Screens and dividers neatly provide a solution by allowing personal spaces and the detritus of everyday life to be hidden out of sight when necessary, while still allowing that all-important feeling of space and freedom of movement to remain.

Specialist manufacturers have come up with attractive solutions. Stiffened or weighted panels that glide along barely seen channels set into the ceiling, stacking up like a pack of cards when not in use, are now available. Draw rods or pulley systems operated by a cord or even an electric motor prevent the leading edges becoming grubby through handling. These panels suit the minimalist, modern character of today's pared-down interiors and can be layered to create different effects and degrees of translucency. And, as they are usually attached to the gliding system with Velcro/touch-and-close tape, they can be easily changed with the seasons.

Variations on this theme might include Venetian, vertical or roller blinds. But if panels or blinds are too austere for your tastes, or for the rest of the room scheme, it is equally feasible to use any style of reversible curtain – remember the dividers will be seen from both sides. In fact, the modern, relaxed styles of heading, such as loops or ties, are perfect for this as they have no 'wrong' side.

SHEERS

Sheers were once, at best, the lacy first line of defence against the destructive forces of sunlight and smog lurking at every Victorian householder's (heavily dressed) windows. At worst, they were the twitching, greying nylon screen behind which nosey neighbours hid.

Now, happily, sheers stand alone as desirable window treatments in their own right, with a vast selection of natural fibres to choose from. In the form of curtains, especially, sheers are essentially feminine, floaty confections that add softness to a room scheme. To play down on their girlie connotations, team them with masculine poles and tiebacks, reduce the amount of fabric used or consider coloured sheers in muted, earthy tones.

this page Sheer fabrics with embroidered motifs are available, but you can add your own trimmings with ribbons and fringing.

opposite, above left Tiny bows of coloured ribbon have been hand-stitched to this plain cotton curtain.

opposite, above right Two-styles-in-one: the hem of the sheer on the left has been dip-dyed to create an irregular border of colour, while the sheer on the right is a self-patterned voile that has been machine-dyed solid yellow.

opposite, below left This embroidered sari has been dyed pink to fill a girlie bedroom with a rosy glow.

opposite, below right Delicate machine-embroidered dragonflies are scattered across this sun-filled space.

Although sheer curtains are the ideal solution when privacy or disguising an unattractive view are the main issues, rather than light, heat or noise insulation, bear in mind that where they are to remain closed, the more gathered the material, the less light that will penetrate into the room. Lightly gathered curtains, minimal flat panels or carefully made blinds (remember every seam will be highlighted against the window) are a useful compromise where the window architecture deserves to be on show but the view doesn't. However, they do have the disadvantage that at night, with a light on, they will quite revealingly live up to their name, so secondary curtains or a plain roller blind mounted close to the window frame might be an additional requirement.

For a lightweight sheer fabric to work as a blind or panel it will need to be stiffened or weighted down in some way. Many blind makers will treat client-supplied fabrics with special chemicals to stiffen the material before making up.

far left Fabrics don't have to be called 'sheers' to do the job. This lightweight gingham, made up into a simple Swedish blind, is semi-translucent and makes the most of available light through this small but sunny window.

left Clouds of embroidered muslin/ voile positively glow in this garden room. Lightweight materials are best suited to simple headings like the tape ties used here with an inexpensive garden cane.

above An antique lace wedding veil has been reinvented as a curtain screen, with a quirky 'pelmet/valance' made of a bundle of twigs secured with twine. The sheer fabric enhances the beauty of the leaded windows.

appliquéd half-panel

Only the minimum of screening is needed for privacy at this nineteenth-century window. A simple geometrically patterned panel decorated with hand-appliquéd motifs accentuates the cobalt glass border and the elegant shape of the frame. This technique is usually associated with folk-art quilts and patchwork, but used sparingly, as here, it can have a much more contemporary feel.

MATERIALS AND EQUIPMENT
pencil and tracing paper
thin cardboard
white cotton sheeting or dressmaking fabric
checked fabric panel (such as gingham)
matching sewing thread
basic sewing kit

1 Enlarge the flower and leaf templates (right) as necessary. Trace off the solid outlines, transfer them onto thin cardboard and cut out.

2 Using a dressmaker's pen, draw round the cardboard onto the cotton fabric. Draw a second line 5mm (¼in) further in, following the broken line on the template. This represents the seam allowance. Add the centre veins to the leaf and cut out the shape.

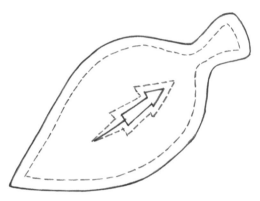

3 Snip into the curved edges at approximately 8mm (⅜in) intervals so that they will lie flat. Cut small notches into the outside curves and clip into the inside curves, ending just outside the pen line. Cut out the centre of the leaf as indicated.

4 Carefully turn under the seam allowance as far as the line, pressing it into place between finger and thumb. Tack/baste down using small stitches. Fold over the surplus fabric at the point and stem of the leaf.

5 Pin and tack/baste the flowers and leaves in position on the panel, so that one motif will hang in front of each pane. Sew down by hand using neat slip stitches. Press lightly using a pressing cloth and hang at the window.

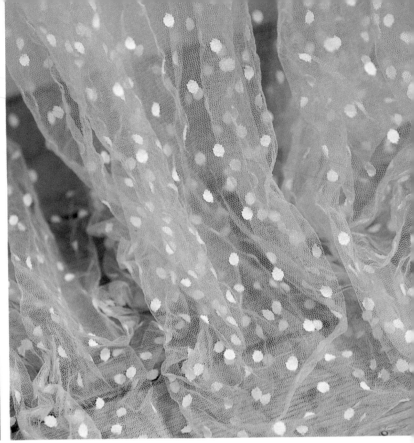

Alternatively, there are various do-it-yourself kits relying on aerosol sprays that can be used at home. Solutions that could add weight and definition to flimsy fabrics include: a contrasting edging made from a heavier fabric stitched along the hem or around all four sides to make a frame; one or more narrow poles hidden in horizontal pockets; a border of heavy trimming along the lower edges; appliqué-style decoration; or even old-fashioned curtain weights sewn into the hem. Which ever method you use, remember these are very lightweight fabrics so don't go overboard, otherwise the fabric will only end up distorted.

For all sheer curtains, but especially for white or off-white fabrics, washability should be an important consideration since such fabrics are prone to gather dust and will soon begin to look dingy (reminiscent of the grey nylons of old). For this reason, if the fabric is not pre-shrunk, machine wash it on the correct cycle before making up your curtains or make allowance for future shrinkage when calculating the measurements. It will also be helpful to choose a heading or style of blind that can easily be undone to allow for regular laundering – softly pleated blinds or curtains with tie-top headings for instance.

opposite Dressmaking fabric ranges include some inspirational sheers like this prettily spotted net which, away from its intended setting, manages to not look overtly bridal. Using a transparent fabric over a background wall colour will alter the end result. Generally pastel colours work best with white sheers, though this mid-apricot creates an interesting effect. Allowing the curtain to 'puddle' on the floor enhances the feminine look.

this page The design of this delicate silk paisley is shown off to great effect when lit from behind. A beaded trim along the leading edge adds definition and structure.

bordered sheer panel

A minimal look works well in a period interior. The clean lines of this bordered panel complement the architectural detail of the Victorian townhouse window and are a welcome modern alternative to a gathered net. The striped frame is mitred at the corners and made in two layers so the panel can be reversed.

MATERIALS AND EQUIPMENT
sheer fabric
striped upholstery fabric
matching sewing thread
ruler
curtain clips
basic sewing kit

MEASURING UP
A = width of frame
B = from bottom of pole to 5cm (2in) below bottom edge of window

CUTTING OUT
Match the stripes exactly on the border strips, so they meet up at the corners.

main panel:
width = A minus 15cm (6in) for border
length = B minus 15cm (6in) for border
Mark a point 1.5cm (½in) in from each corner.

long borders (cut 4):
width = 11cm (4in)
length = A plus 3cm (1in) for seams

short borders (cut 4):
width = 11cm (4in)
length = B plus 3cm (1in) for seams

1 The ends of the borders are trimmed at 45 degrees. Working on the wrong side, mark a point along what will be the inside edge of the first short border, 11cm (4in) in from the left corner. Using a dressmaker's pen, draw a line up to the other corner and cut along it. Shape the other corners, making sure that all the inside edges are the same colour.

2 Lightly press and unfold a 1.5cm (½in) seam allowance along both short edges and the longest edge of each border panel.

3 With right sides together, pin and tack/baste the inside edge of a short border to the top of the panel. Line the creases up with the dots at the corners. Turn over, then pin and tack/baste a second short border to the other side, so the right side faces downwards.

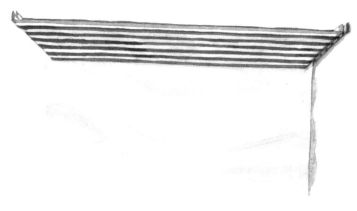

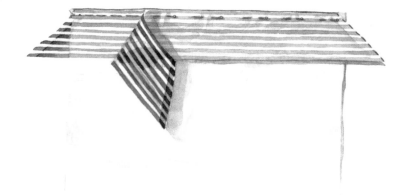

4 Machine stitch through all three layers, 1.5cm (½in) from the edge. Refold the seam allowance at the ends of the two borders and press the strips away from the panel.

5 Attach the other two short and the four long border strips in the same way. Clip off the surplus fabric at each corner 5mm (¼in) from the corner.

6 Refold the seam allowance along the outside edges of the border strips. Pin and tack/baste the seam allowance under all the way round the border.

7 Join the mitred corners on both sides of the panel with slip stitch, sewing from the outer edge of the corner inwards.

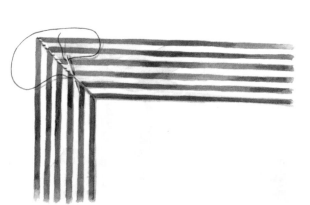

8 Tack/baste the two borders together around the outside, tucking in any surplus fabric at the corners. Machine stitch 3mm (⅛in) from the edge. Press the panel and attach to the curtain rod with metal clips.

DETAILS

Just as the right accessories will transform an understated little black dress into a showstopper, so well-chosen poles, finials, tiebacks, trimmings and headings can transform simple or inexpensive window treatments into individual, characterful and eye-catching features. But use these details with restraint – remember, there's nothing worse than looking over-dressed!

Sometimes these 'accessories' are pure serendipity: lucky hand-me-downs and antique-shop finds; sometimes they come from an afternoon's research in a specialist shop – don't limit yourself to retailers dedicated to interiors though, look in dress departments, too, where potential crossovers include sequins, sari ribbons and lace edgings. Alternatively, pure invention comes into play, transforming found objects like driftwood, sea shells, sea glass and 'witches' stones' (the beach pebbles with holes through the middle) into curtain 'jewellery'.

Remember that the plainer the curtain fabric and style, the more the tieback, trim or finial will clamour for attention. Conversely, the more decorative the curtain, the less these details will be noticed.

opposite, above left Simple white drapes with a fixed heading over an arched doorway are elevated from the ordinary with the addition of handmade cut-out leaf covers to hide the tiebacks and heading hooks.

opposite, above right An ornate carved and gilded finial steals the show when partnered with a plain wooden pole and understated plaid cotton curtains.

opposite, below left An opulent pewter tassel can transcend period styling in a resolutely contemporary interior.

opposite, below right Coordinated bobble fringing adds texture while maintaining the naturalistic style of these calico/muslin curtains.

this page Casual observers might miss these charming fossil knobs, the only decoration on a rough silk panel, but once spotted they lend character to the otherwise minimalist styling.

opposite The traditional styles of heading, like these neat triple pleats, really show their pedigree when the curtains are opened and closed, gliding, as they do, with the folds of fabric falling into regimented order.

this page These room dividers make the point that screening does not have to stretch from floor to ceiling in order to be effective. An inventive arrangement of bent copper rods attached through metal eyelets in the fabric both suspends the frayed panels of linen from the ceiling and weights them at floor level. The result offers privacy and demarcation while allowing light from the windows to spill from one area of the open-plan space to another.

headings

Today, the trend for simple and lightly gathered curtains has, in many situations, overshadowed the role of more complicated, ornate headings like hand-stitched goblet pleats, lattice pleats and box pleats. However, these formal styles should not be dismissed as 'old-fashioned' or 'too fussy'. They still have the ability to add that special 'something' that is both the perfect foil to the most expensive fabrics and a way of adding glamour to the cheapest. And as many of the traditional headings can now be replicated with specialist ready-made gathering tapes, there is no excuse not to go the extra length, should the situation demand it.

Of the straightforward gathering tapes, the most versatile options are narrow gathering tape, which replicates a drawstring effect and is only suitable for small or lightweight curtains such as sheers; pencil-pleat tape, which creates an even row of small parallel pleats, for use on medium- to heavyweight fabrics; and deep pencil-pleat tape, which is similar to pencil-pleat tape but has more cords to create a fuller, more stylized gather. A trick worth considering when using narrow gathering tape is to fix it 10cm (4in) or more below the top of the curtain (remember to include this additional amount when calculating the overall length), which results in an attractively casual, floppy top edge.

Another traditional but relatively unfussy treatment is the café-style 'slot' heading that can be used for full- or half-length curtains. For this style, a channel is stitched along the top of the curtain panel through which the pole or curtain wire is threaded. The gathered heading is then effectively fixed, with the curtains being held back when necessary with a tie- or holdback. Again, this channel can be positioned below the top of the curtain to create a soft edging along the top edge.

Beyond the traditional styles, the more contemporary innovations combine the function of heading, hook and curtain ring in one. Simple tabs constructed from the curtain fabric are either looped over the pole or held in place with buttons or Velcro/touch-and-close tape. This style works well with panels that hang flat or in loose gathers when closed. Similar, but more pretty and feminine, are tie-on headings, which can be practically any width, from narrow and neat to broad and flouncy.

For instant, no-sew curtains, curtain clips are heaven-sent. Available in a range of metallic finishes and strengths, they can transform simple hemmed panels, antique quilts, plaid blankets, lacy tablecloths and saris – in fact, any approximately rectangular piece of fabric – into an instant curtain. If the panel is too long, merely fold the top over to create an integral pelmet/valance.

More high-tech in appearance are metal eyelets, which come in several diameters, the narrowest of which could be hung over hooks on the wall for a semi-fixed panel or strung from tension wire, while the largest are big enough to thread straight onto a narrow curtain pole.

An advantage of these contemporary heading styles is that they don't have a wrong side. This means that should you want to use a double-sided fabric or a lined panel – which has the bonus of improving the view of the window when seen from the outside – you can ring the changes with the seasons or your moods by simply reversing the way it is hung.

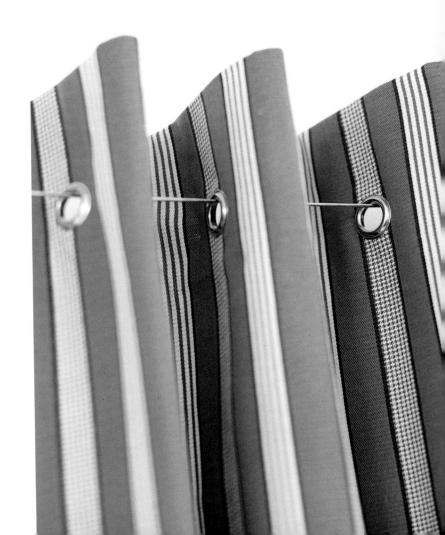

near right Loosely gathered pencil pleats married with a smart damask look formal but not too traditional.

centre right For an unobtrusive heading, run a double hem along the top and add ties made from the same fabric as the curtains.

far right Traditional hand-sewn pleats take on a contemporary look in unbleached linen.

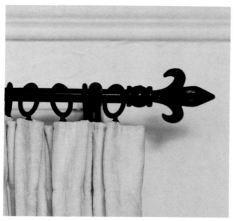

left Metal eyelets suspended from a tension wire create a nautical look with a blue and white stripe fabric.

above Is it a curtain or is it a blind? Edging calico/muslin with jute tape provides a sturdy frame for a fixed-headed panel – a simple variation on a Roman blind.

right Positioning ordinary gathering tape well below the top of the curtain creates a casual, floppy effect and helps disguise an unattractive track or pole.

jasmine-headed curtain

This charming, quirky curtain, described by its maker as a 'quick fix', requires the bare minimum of sewing. It was created by simply folding a double length of fabric in half and attaching twig circlets – available from craft suppliers or florists – to the top edge in place of curtain rings. Lengths of realistic silk jasmine flowers wind through the rings and act as a tieback to complete the natural theme. The effect is theatrical and ideally suited to a doorway such as this, which is in constant use, so the curtain is drawn back at all times.

MATERIALS AND EQUIPMENT
heavy cotton fabric
matching sewing thread
silk embroidery thread/floss
large crewel needle
twig circlets
silk jasmine flowers
tieback hook
drill, screws and rawlplugs/plugs
basic sewing kit

MEASURING UP
A = width of doors or window plus 40cm (16in)
B = from bottom of rings to floor

CUTTING OUT
Using a flat seam, join lengths of fabric to the required width. Ensure the selvedges lie on the outside edges to avoid having to make side hems.

width = 1½ x A
length = 3 x B

1 Run a 2cm (¾in) double hem along the top and bottom edges.

2 Lay the fabric out on the floor and fold in half lengthways with wrong sides together. This will be easier if you have somebody to help you manoeuvre the fabric.

3 Using a dressmaker's pen and starting at the leading-edge corner, mark the positions for the rings along the top. They should be at intervals of about 20cm (8in).

4 Cut a long length of embroidery silk/floss and thread all six strands through a large crewel needle. Leaving the end loose, sew the first circlet in place by passing the needle through the top edge of the curtain and between the outer twigs three times.

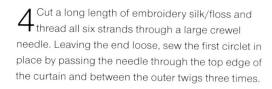

5 Knot the two ends securely. Wrap the loose thread firmly around the loop, then tie off and trim the ends, leaving two short 'tails'. Attach the rest of the circlets in the same way, then hang the curtain.

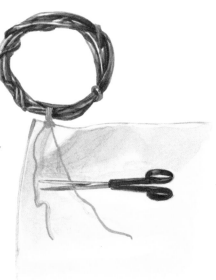

6 Weave lengths of silk flowers through the circlets to form loops. Allow the ends to trail down over the curtain.

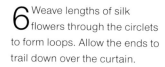

7 Screw the tieback hook to the adjacent wall about halfway down the door. Tie the curtain back with the remaining lengths of jasmine and fix them over the hook.

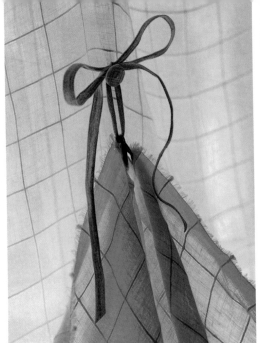

tiebacks and holdbacks

Although on the receiving end of some bad press of late for their somewhat prissy lineage, tiebacks have practical as well as decorative advantages even in today's laid-back rooms. They are a must, for instance, at French windows, where the curtains would inevitably flap in the breeze without them. They are also necessary for fixed or false curtains, where the objective is to make the window treatment look as full and realistic as possible. In fact, any curtain which needs to be restrained if the window or opening is not to be obscured – including door curtains, heavily gathered drapes designed to hang in decorative folds and bed curtains – all need to be held back in some way for some, if not all, of the time.

The most attractive of the traditional styles for holdbacks are plain or decorative metal cloak pins and u-shaped brackets. Cloak pins are metal or wooden disks mounted on a short rod which is fixed to the wall or window surround. The old-fashioned bracket-style holdbacks actually sit particularly well with the present vogue for metal poles and rings.

Other traditional styles to take inspiration from include large tassels hung from cord, which can look very grand in silk but quite relaxed in humbler materials such as cotton or jute.

opposite, main and far left A functional black-painted metal hook is the perfect foil for the informally draped linen sheet at the window of this sun-drenched room. A second sheet has been cleverly nailed in position on the beams to act as a pelmet/valance, equally in keeping with the relaxed atmosphere of the setting.

opposite, centre left This printed sheer curtain has been gathered up in soft folds and 'gift wrapped' with an rosette of dark translucent ribbon.

opposite, centre right The bottom corner of this sheer linen panel can be held up during the day by looping the simple tape bow over an antique button which has been sewn on just below the heading.

opposite, right A piece of tartan ribbon has been stitched to the centre of a wider length of pink taffeta ribbon and tied around a gauzy curtain to make an informal tieback, reminiscent of a Scottish country dancer's sash.

right Sometimes the traditional favourites are still the best choice: this silky rope tieback with its coordinating bullion tassel adds a classic touch to a pink velvet curtain.

below right This sculptural brass holdback, fixed at sill height, is an elegant and unobtrusive way of keeping the folds of a heavy linen curtain in place. This treatment would work equally well in a period or modern interior.

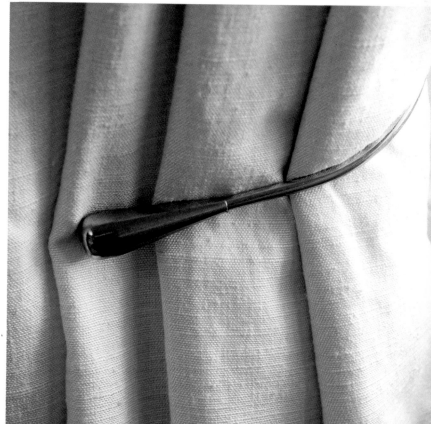

Crescent-shaped, reinforced fabric tiebacks and fabric plaits, bows and rosettes are now arguably in the same camp as Austrian blinds: irredeemable and best avoided!

Otherwise, be inventive and choose a tieback which will complement your curtain. Something as simple as a piece of rope with a loop at either end to fix onto a wall hook or a loose length of ribbon would do the job stylishly without looking too contrived. Or what about a silk scarf, salvaged doorknob, leather belt or chunky vintage necklace (pearls look stunning with a sheer fabric, while wooden beads make a sweet partner to a cheery gingham)?

It is a good idea to fix your tiebacks in place after the curtains have been hung at the window, having first experimented with different positions. They should be positioned directly below the end of the track or pole and as a rule they should be roughly two-thirds of the way down floor-to-ceiling curtains, so that the fabric will be pulled back in an elegant curve. If the tiebacks are placed higher up, more of the window will be revealed and the room will be lighter, but the proportions are not always so pleasing. If they are lower, the curtains will hang in fuller, more theatrical folds.

padded holdback

The deep folds of this silk curtain are restrained with a padded cloak-pin, giving an extravagant, sculpted appearance. The woodwork can be avoided by simply covering a ready-made holdback.

1 Sand the disc and dowelling to remove any sharp edges. Drill a hole through the centre of the disc and into both ends of the dowelling.

2 Press a 1cm (½in) hem along one edge of the fabric square and stick down with adhesive. Coat the wrong side with adhesive and leave until almost dry. Wrap the fabric around the dowelling with the hem on the outside edge and a 1cm (½in) overlap at each end. Trim the overlap to 5mm (¼in).

MATERIALS AND EQUIPMENT
10cm (4in) disc of 2cm (⅔in) MDF
10cm (4in) length of 2cm (⅔in) dowelling
sandpaper
drill
fabric
PVA adhesive
5cm (2in) screw
thick polyester wadding/batting
buttonhole/button thread
double-ended screw (available from specialist hardware shops)
rawlplug/plug (if necessary)
screwdriver
basic sewing kit

CUTTING OUT
fabric:
12cm (5in) square
25cm (10in) circle

wadding:
7.5cm (3in) circle
10cm (4in) circle
15cm (6in) circle

3 Screw the disc to one end of the dowelling. Glue the medium-sized circle of wadding to the disc, then glue the smallest circle on top of this.

4 Tack/baste a 1cm (½in) turning around the outside edge of the fabric circle. Using buttonhole thread, sew a round of running stitch just inside the raw edge, leaving a length of thread at each end. Pin and tack/baste the remaining wadding centrally to the wrong side of the fabric circle.

6 Fix the double-ended screw to the end of the dowelling. Attach the holdback to the window surround or wall, using a Rawlplug if it is to be fixed into plaster.

5 Place the fabric over the disc and draw up the gathers around the dowelling. Ease the turning to the wrong side, then knot the ends of the thread and sew them through the fabric to secure the gathers.

this page Binding the top and bottom of the integral pelmet/valance on these sheers with narrow scarlet ribbon both highlights its presence and draws attention to the meringue-like fullness of the curtains.

opposite, above left This luxurious tasselled fringe is shown to great effect against a subtle cream-on-cream crewel-work fabric.

opposite, above centre A labour of love, this intricate scalloped leading edge would take hours to make, but creates a dramatic feature, especially against the pale curtain fabric.

opposite, above right A military-style stripe is achieved by using two different widths of braid sewn on top of one another.

opposite, below A trimming should be heavy enough in comparison with the curtain fabric to bring definition to the shape, but not so heavy as to distort it. Here a lightweight bobble fringe works well with a flimsy voile.

trims and decorations

In the category of curtain details, the trimmings offer the greatest scope for imagination – and fun. Of the ready-made options, ribbons are the most understated, timeless and inexpensive (trimmings can easily cost more per metre than the fabrics). With their near relatives, patterned braids, ribbons come in all manner of fabrics, including velvet, satin, silk, organza and wool, and you needn't restrict yourself to those made for soft furnishings. Endlessly versatile, they can be fashioned into tiebacks, tie-tops, edgings, or to hide a seam where two different fabrics are joined.

Fringes, either cut, tasselled, beaded, bobble or twisted bullion, come in every style, from short and discrete to downright shaggy and attention-grabbing. They work best used along the leading edge of generously gathered curtains, where not only is the fringe seen to best advantage, but attention can be drawn to the fullness of the curve. Fringes also work well as an embellishment to the bottom of a pelmet/valance or blind. Indeed, rows of fringing sewn along every section of a Roman blind look amazing when the blind is pleated up – like a 1920s flapper's dress.

Unsurprisingly, the offbeat approach to curtains has infiltrated the realm of trimmings. Quirky ideas include sequins and antique pearl or horn buttons scattered along hems and leading edges. Trims needn't add a luxurious or stylized effect – found objects like shells and feathers sewn along a ribbon can make delicate homemade trims and capture the trend for all things natural.

zigzag pelmet/valance

Pelmets/valances were traditionally used to hide curtain tracks, but this updated version adds visual interest to the top of a plain Roman blind. When the blind is fully up, the pleats are hidden by the zigzag edging. The exact size and shape of the triangles will depend on the width of your window frame; cut out a full-sized version in paper to check that the proportions work before you start sewing.

MAKING THE TEMPLATE

Work out the width of the triangular points by dividing the width of the pelmet/valance by the number required – a 90cm (36in) wide window will require ten 9cm (3½in) triangles. Cut an equilateral triangle from thin card, with each side equal to this measurement. If you prefer to have longer, narrower points, simply make your template into an isosceles triangle, with two longer, equal sides. (The simplest way to do this is to draw a baseline of the required width; set a compass to the required depth of the points and mark off the apex of the triangle with the compass positioned at either end of the baseline in turn.) Draw a vertical line down the centre of the template to divide it in half.

MATERIALS AND EQUIPMENT

pencil

thin card

compass/drawing compass and long ruler/yardstick

plain/solid fabric

matching sewing thread

2cm (⅔in) wide Velcro/touch-and-close tape

basic sewing kit

for the board:

3 x 10cm (1¼in x 4in) wood or 2D, the width of window frame plus 5cm (2in) overlap at each side

sandpaper

paint to match fabric

2 angle brackets

screwdriver, drill, rawlplugs/plugs and screws

staple gun

CUTTING OUT

cut front and back alike

width = width of board plus 22cm (9in)

depth = 22cm (9in)

1 Sand the board and paint it to match the fabric. When dry, screw the two angle brackets to the underside, 10cm (4in) in from each end.

2 Cut a length of Velcro/tape to fit around the sides and front edge. Separate the two pieces and staple the hooked side around the front and sides of the board. Fix the board in place above the window using rawlplugs/plugs.

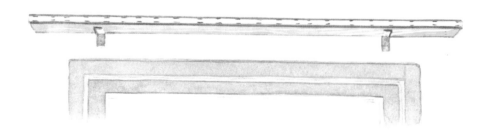

3 Mark the seam allowance on the wrong side of the back panel: using a dressmaker's pen and a long ruler/yardstick, draw three lines 1cm (½in) in from the sides and the bottom edge.

4 Starting at the bottom left corner, match the centre and base of the template up to the lines. Draw along the right edge of the template, then draw a series of triangles along the bottom line, ending with another half-triangle.

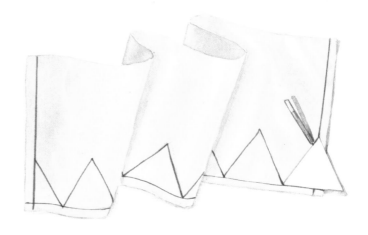

5 Pin the front and back panels together with right sides together, then tack/baste along the sides and close to the zigzag line.

6 Stitch along the drawn lines, then cut away the excess fabric, snipping in between the triangles and clipping the points so they will lie flat. Turn right sides out, easing the points into shape with a knitting needle. Press, then machine stitch all around the seam 3mm (⅛in) from the edge.

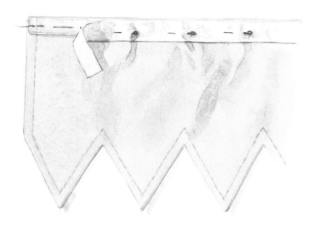

7 Tack/baste the top edges together, then press under a 1cm (½in) turning. Pin and tack/baste the remaining strip of Velcro/tape over the raw edges. Machine stitch down along the top and bottom edges of the Velcro/tape. Start both rows of stitching from the same edge to prevent the fabric from puckering.

8 Mount the pelmet/valance onto the board, carefully matching up the two pieces of Velcro/tape.

ruched pelmet/valance

Crisp cotton and natural linen are combined to make this simple pelmet/valance. It is gathered onto a sprung wire and hung in front of a sheer white curtain. The double heading creates a decorative ruffle, which also conceals a utilitarian roller blind that gives added privacy to the room.

MATERIALS AND EQUIPMENT
white cotton fabric
unbleached linen
matching sewing thread
long ruler/yardstick
pencil
bradawl/awl
2 screw-eyes and 2 cup hooks
sprung curtain wire
wire cutters
basic sewing kit

MEASURING UP AND CUTTING OUT
The measurements are for a valance approximately 40cm (16in) deep; adjust them accordingly for a taller or shorter window.

cotton panel:
width = 2 x width of window
depth = 53cm (21in)

linen border:
width = 2 x width of window
depth = 18cm (7in)

1 Pin the border to the panel along one long edge with wrong sides facing. Tack/baste, then machine stitch 8mm (⅜in) from the edge. Trim the seam allowance back to 6mm (¼in).

2 Refold the seam so the raw edges are enclosed and press lightly along the stitch line. Machine 8mm (⅜in) from the fold to make a French seam. Press the seam allowance downwards.

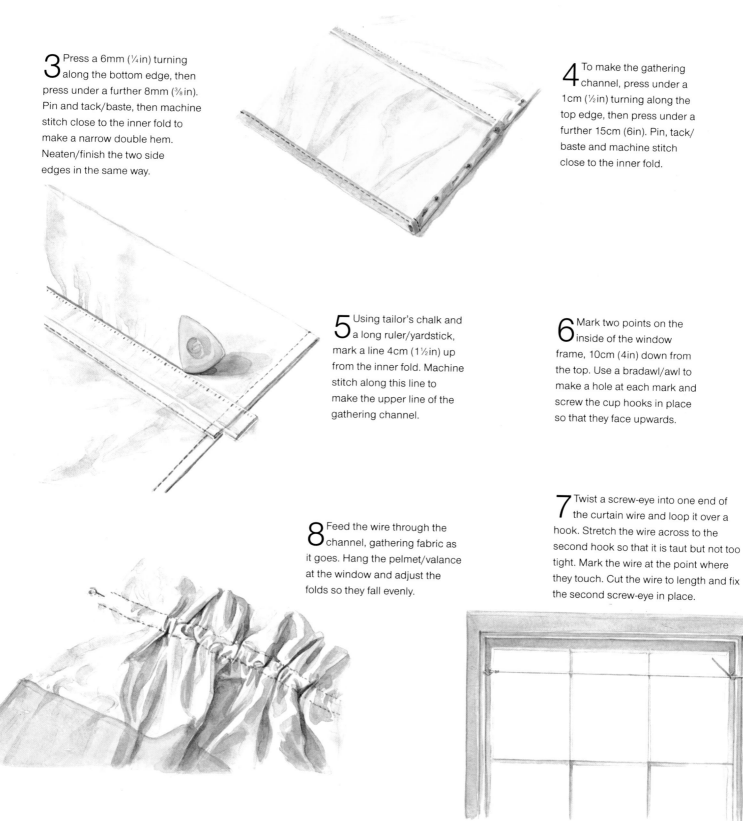

3 Press a 6mm (¼in) turning along the bottom edge, then press under a further 8mm (⅜in). Pin and tack/baste, then machine stitch close to the inner fold to make a narrow double hem. Neaten/finish the two side edges in the same way.

4 To make the gathering channel, press under a 1cm (½in) turning along the top edge, then press under a further 15cm (6in). Pin, tack/baste and machine stitch close to the inner fold.

5 Using tailor's chalk and a long ruler/yardstick, mark a line 4cm (1½in) up from the inner fold. Machine stitch along this line to make the upper line of the gathering channel.

6 Mark two points on the inside of the window frame, 10cm (4in) down from the top. Use a bradawl/awl to make a hole at each mark and screw the cup hooks in place so that they face upwards.

7 Twist a screw-eye into one end of the curtain wire and loop it over a hook. Stretch the wire across to the second hook so that it is taut but not too tight. Mark the wire at the point where they touch. Cut the wire to length and fix the second screw-eye in place.

8 Feed the wire through the channel, gathering fabric as it goes. Hang the pelmet/valance at the window and adjust the folds so they fall evenly.

room by room

LIVING SPACES

KITCHENS

BEDROOMS

CHILDREN'S ROOMS

BATHROOMS

below, right and far right This row of neutral linen curtains disguises different window styles. Hanging them in front of a narrow fabric-covered pelmet/valance adds to the tailored effect.

opposite, centre and below A silk stripe is used for this pleated and swagged pelmet/valance and also edges the semi-sheer silk curtains, creating a frame around the attractive sash window.

LIVING SPACES

The living space is by definition the place we spend most of our leisure time at home, whether alone, with family or entertaining. It is also likely to have the largest windows: curved or three-sided bays, floor-to-ceiling sashes and French windows traditionally characterize the most prestigious rooms in a home.

For these reasons, the window treatments in your living space – whether they be flowing drapes or minimal tailored blinds – should make a dramatic statement, while suiting the decorative style of the room. It makes sense to lavish most thought on the curtains and blinds you choose for these rooms because if there's a mistake, it's likely as not going to be a public – and expensive – one.

In today's informal homes with their open-plan layouts, most living spaces – the double living rooms typical of old terraced houses/row houses, for instance – must meet the requirements of both a family room and a formal reception room. That is to say they need to look formal yet cosy and be smart yet resilient enough to take the rough and tumble of everyday life.

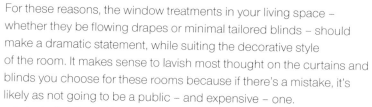

this page Cream damask drapes are a subtle but luxurious foil to the dominating architecture of the verandah seen beyond the window.

opposite, main picture Lengths of lilac voile doubled over a pole and dressed with a wool shawl make an instant window treatment in this bohemian apartment.

opposite, above right These almost transparent white Swedish blinds preserve the striking window architecture and the monochrome decorating scheme of this chic loft apartment.

opposite, centre right Allowing full-length drapes to fall in soft folds on the floor creates an impractical but luxurious effect, easily justified in a formal room.

opposite, below right Panels of plain colour can be used vertically as well as horizontally to create interesting effects. Here lighter-coloured panels are used to create additional screening during the day in this well-lit room. Positioning the darker panels on the outside of the window creates a framing effect.

Roman blind

This type of Roman blind is made from a lined rectangular panel, weighted by a lath, with cords on the reverse side. It is hung from a batten, which can be fixed in a window recess or mounted on a wall. A closely woven cotton fabric such as ticking is easy to sew and will endure heavy use.

MATERIALS AND EQUIPMENT
white lining fabric
ticking or similar striped fabric
long ruler/yardstick
1.5cm (½in) plastic rings
matching sewing thread
wooden lath, 2cm (¾in) shorter
than finished width of blind
3 x 3cm (1¼ x 1¼in) wooden
batten/wooden lathe, 5mm (¼in)
shorter than finished width of blind
drill, screwdriver and
rawlplugs/plugs
3 small screw-eyes
staple gun
nylon blind cord
small safety pin
blind acorn/pull
cleat and screws
basic sewing kit

if blind is to hang in a window
recess:
4 long screws and rawlplugs/plugs

if blind is to hang outside a window
recess or over a frame:
2 small angle brackets, screws and
rawlplugs/plugs
If the blind is to be mounted on the
wall, the ends and underside of the
batten/wooden strip will be visible,
so the wood should be painted to
match the colour of the blind.

MEASURING UP
if blind is to hang in a window
recess:
A = width of recess minus 2cm (¾in)
B = from top of recess to sill

if blind is to hang outside a window
recess or over a frame:
A = width of frame or recess plus
6cm (2½in)
B = from top of batten to 3cm (1¼in)
below bottom edge of frame or sill

CUTTING OUT
blind and lining alike:
width = A plus 4cm (1½in)
depth= B plus 12cm (5in)

3 cords cut to the following lengths:
2B; 2B plus ¼A; 2B plus A

1 Using tailor's chalk, mark a line down the centre of the right side of the lining, then draw two more lines 5cm (2in) in from each long edge. Starting 15cm (6in) up from the bottom edge, mark a series of 30cm (12in) intervals along each line. Leave a space of at least 20cm (8in) at the top edge to accommodate the blind when it is drawn up.

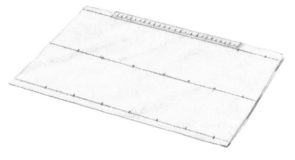

2 Hand stitch a small plastic ring securely to each of the marks, then brush away the chalk lines.

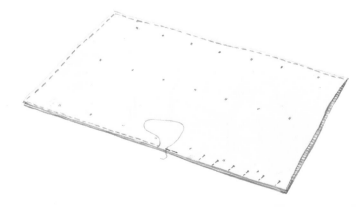

3 With right sides together, pin together the long side edges and top edge of the blind and the lining. Tack/baste, then machine stitch, leaving a seam allowance of 2cm (¾in). Clip the corners, turn right-side out and press.

4 Make a casing to hold the lath at the bottom of the blind on the same side as the rings. Press under a 2cm (¾in) turning along the raw edge, then press under a further 4cm (1¼in) turning. Tack/baste down, then machine stitch 3mm (⅛in) from the inside fold.

5 Slip the lath inside the casing and use slip stitch to secure the open ends.

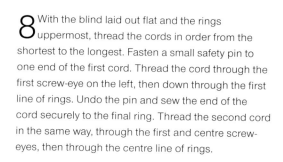

6 If the blind is to fit in a recess, drill four equally spaced holes through the batten/wooden strip from top to bottom. Mark the centre back of the batten/wooden strip. Then fix the screw-eyes to the underside so that one will lie at the top of each line of rings.

7 Press a 2cm (¾in) fold to the wrong side along the blind's top edge. With the right side of the blind facing down, staple the centre top of the blind to the centre back of the batten/wooden strip, so that the fold lies along the back edge of the batten. Continue stapling towards each end: the fabric will overlap the batten/wooden strip slightly.

8 With the blind laid out flat and the rings uppermost, thread the cords in order from the shortest to the longest. Fasten a small safety pin to one end of the first cord. Thread the cord through the first screw-eye on the left, then down through the first line of rings. Undo the pin and sew the end of the cord securely to the final ring. Thread the second cord in the same way, through the first and centre screw-eyes, then through the centre line of rings.

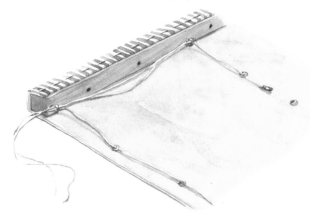

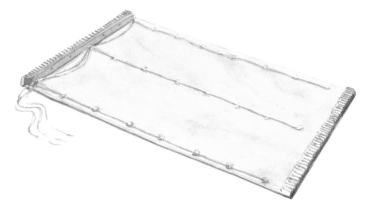

9 Attach the third cord in the same way, passing it through the preceding screw-eyes. Thread all the loose ends through the acorn and adjust them so that they are the same length. Knot securely, trim and slide the acorn/pull over the knot. (For a blind that pulls up from the left, start with the first screw-eye on the right.)

10 A wall-mounted blind is fixed on or above the window frame, using a small angle bracket at each end of the batten. If the blind is to fit in a window recess, drill four holes into the top of the recess in line with the holes in the batten and use long screws and rawlplugs/plugs to fix it in place. Screw a cleat on or near the frame, on the same side as the cords.

It is possible, given a large enough room, to have designated 'ends' so that formal and informal areas are, to a certain extent, self-contained, with the appropriate window treatment used for each – say luxurious, swaggy curtains at one window and a tailored blind, in the same fabric for continuity, at the other. Dividing curtains or a folding screen would reinforce the two-rooms-in-one approach without losing the feeling of space.

The other dual-purpose aspect of a living space is that it will probably be used with equal frequency during the day and night, so whatever fabric you opt for should be tested in both natural and artificial light before purchase. Similarly, the proposed style of curtain or blind should be assessed for its suitability both open and drawn (or up and down).

Because most living rooms are at the front of the building, facing the street or public approach, how they look from the outside as well as the inside may be another consideration, for the rather dull rule that linings should be plain doesn't hold sway any longer, especially as more attractive alternatives – a smart ticking for instance – can be had at pretty much the same price.

main picture A tailored Roman blind is a smart and practical treatment for this window set above a day bed.

left Customizing these plain cream curtains with a boldly scalloped edge lifts them above the ordinary and draws the eye to the view beyond.

opposite, above right Using one continuous pole with differently sized pairs of tailored drapes meets the challenges of this combination of French doors and side windows.

opposite, below right The contrasting band of paler (and more densely woven) fabric in these linen curtains makes an elegant statement and could be an inventive way to reinvent old curtains for a taller window.

ribbon-trimmed lined curtains

These plain curtains have been transformed with an extravagant satin lining and a velvet-ribbon trim. They are slightly over-long so the folds spill onto the polished floor, increasing the feeling of opulence. The French pleats are created with a ready-made heading tape, but if you prefer a handmade finish, follow the method given on pages 59–61.

MATERIALS AND EQUIPMENT

plain/solid fabric

contrasting satin lining

2.5cm (1in) and 8cm (3in) wide velvet ribbon

matching sewing thread

pencil

French-pleat heading tape

long ruler/yardstick and set square/carpenter's square

pronged curtain hooks

basic sewing kit

MEASURING UP

A = ½ length of curtain pole

B = from bottom of curtain rings to floor plus 13cm (5 in)

CUTTING OUT

curtain:

width = 2 or 2.5 x A for each curtain, depending on the type of heading tape you have (refer to the manufacturer's instructions). Add to this 12cm (5in) for side turnings plus 10cm (4in) for overlap

length = B plus 8cm (3in) for top hem plus 10cm (4in) for bottom hem

lining:

width = width of curtain panel minus 10cm (4in)

length = B minus 6cm (2½in)

heading tape:

A plus 25cm (10in)

1 Mark the centre top of the curtain and lining fabric with small notches.

2 Press under a 2cm (1in) hem along the bottom of the lining.

3 The ribbon edging runs along the sides and bottom of the curtain. Pin and tack the narrow ribbon 16 cm in from the side edges and 25 cm from the bottom, mitring the corners. Slip stitch down by hand using matching sewing thread. Close the mitres with slip stitch. Apply the wide ribbon in the same way, 10 cm further in.

4 With right sides facing and the top edges matching, pin and tack the sides of the curtain and lining together. Starting at the top corners, machine stitch, leaving a seam allowance of 1 cm to within 20 cm of the bottom edge of the lining.

5 Press the seam allowance lightly towards the centre so it lies flat against the lining fabric, then turn right sides out. Line up the notches on the top edge. Pin and tack from this point outwards to each corner. The seams will now lie 5 cm in from the sides. Press the edges lightly.

6 Press under a 8 cm heading along the top edge. Turn the corners in at a slight angle and press.

7 Gather up the heading tape to find out where the pinch pleats will form. Mark the position of the two outermost pleats with a pencil. Pull the tape flat again and lay it over the top turning. Adjust it so that there is an equal space of approximately 10 cm either side of the outermost pleats, then pin it in place 2 cm down from the top edge. Draw two lines across the tape to mark where it crosses the sides of the curtain.

8 Unthread the gathering cords each end of the tape to 4 cm within the outer pencil line. On the leading edge, knot them securely together on the wrong side, and leave the other cords loose. Cut off the surplus tape along the lines, then press under 1 cm to neaten the ends. Tack, then machine in place, starting each long row of stitching from the same end.

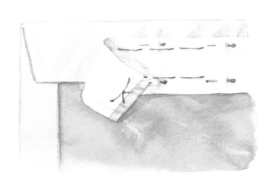

9 Press under and unfold the remaining seam allowance along the sides of the lining, then unfold the hem. Mitre each corner by turning in at a 45-degree angle so that the crease lines match up. Press along the diagonal. Refold the hems, then slip stitch the mitre. Tack/baste down the hem and the unstitched seam allowance at the sides.

10 Double check the length, then press under a 10cm (4in) hem on the curtain. Mitre as for the lining, then pin and tack/ baste down the hem turning. Pin and tack/baste the bottom edge of the lining onto the curtain and slip stitch in place.

11 Pull up the gathering threads to create the pleats. Rather than cut them, wrap the loose ends around a piece of card, so that the curtains can be flattened out for dry cleaning.

12 Depending on the type of tape used, insert a curtain hook or a triple-pin hook at each pleat. To make sure that the three pleats hold together and to give a crisper appearance, you can secure them at the base with a few small stitches.

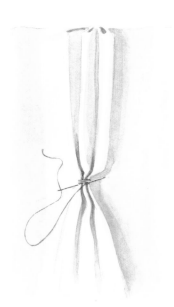

KITCHENS

No longer placed firmly out of sight
'below stairs', the kitchen is now the heart
of the house: the room where the family
both cooks and eats, watches television
and does homework, where everyone
gathers for parties, and likely as not,
where more money has been spent than
on any other home improvement, creating
the 'dream' kitchen which we all seem to
hanker after.

This creates something of a dichotomy. If the kitchen is to
be on show to all and sundry, then the curtains and blinds
need to keep up appearances, but as the kitchen is
essentially a working room, filled with steam and cooking
smells (which will cling to any fabrics present), the window
treatment needs to be practical, too.

In fact, given that the kitchen is not usually a room
where privacy is an issue, it may be that not all windows
will need a treatment at all, especially the small windows
typically found above a worktop or sink, which will be
constantly splashed in any event. Similarly, it will probably
be unnecessary, not to say unwise, to consider a layered
window treatment.

Generally, lightly gathered curtains, café curtains
or simple, tailored blinds are the obvious answer in a
kitchen. For the fabrics, the best options will be washable,
wipeable – oilcloth, for instance, makes great blinds – or
stain-resistant. Where the fabric will be washed – linen
and cotton are, of course, ideal workhorse materials for
kitchens – make allowance for any shrinkage or pre-shrink
the fabric before making up.

Choose simple headings like tab-tops and tie-tops, and
poles that can be easily dismantled for cleaning. You
definitely want to avoid spending hours taking out and
reinserting curtain hooks and adjusting decorative

The unusual striped fabric (combined with
a coordinating linoleum flooring) in this
attractive dining-room-cum-kitchen hits the
perfect balance between practicality and
elegance for a working kitchen that is also
used for entertaining. A blind above the
worktop is a sensible choice, reproduced
above the other window for continuity and
balance. Using a single curtain at the
French doors and anchoring it to the left
of the doorway with a holdback keeps the
fabric away from the worktop.

headings when frequent laundering will be required. Plain/solid or relatively unsophisticated fabrics will look more at ease with the working nature of the room than grand, ornately patterned ones and will better suit the simple style of the heading, too. And bear in mind that constant handling with sticky hands will soon leave a mark, so avoid curtain and blind styles that need lots of 'coaxing' into position.

Don't forget to apply lateral thinking to the problem. Indeed a good solution may be right at hand in the shape of the humble tea towel/dishtowel. Whether modern or antique, tea towels/dishtowels make witty yet eminently sensible kitchen curtains and blinds.

Where the kitchen is part of an open-plan living area, consider treating the room as two (or more) distinct areas linked by a common window-treatment theme. This may involve choosing the same patterned or plain/solid fabric for all the windows, but adapting the styling of the window treatment to suit the function of each area – blinds in the kitchen area and gathered curtains

living area, for example. Here, choosing a fabric that is practical yet sufficiently attractive to look the part sounds challenging, but good-quality natural fabrics like cottons and linens, either plain or in cheerful, timeless designs such as stripes, checks, plaids or florals would fit the bill. And you can always add trimmings and other decorative details, such as an ornate pole or pair of finials, to the treatments in the living area if you feel the need to smarten things up a bit.

opposite, left Wipeable, floor-to-ceiling roller blinds, decorated with rows of tiny holes are a neat, flexible solution in a contemporary kitchen.

opposite, above right Curtains treatments have other uses in kitchens besides screening windows. Here, this simple plaid gathered panel hides the unsightly cleaning materials on an open shelf beneath the sink.

opposite, below right These lightly gathered gingham curtains are purely decorative. Attaching them to the window itself rather than the surrounding frame, means that the window can easily be opened for ventilation.

this page Loosely gathered, pencil-pleat curtains in an inexpensive, washable cotton cambric suit the country style of this open-plan kitchen-dining room.

above Nothing could be simpler, or more breezy, than these white cotton panels pinned up with curtain clips. They remain pristine because they are so easy to take down and launder.

above right Here, a whole length of tea-towel/dishtowel fabric – it was traditionally sold by the yard for housewives to make up into individual cloths – makes an attractive Roman blind. Being of a simple, loose construction,

without any reinforcing poles, the blind can be gently hand-washed, cords and all.

right These fine linen curtains with integral pelmet/valance are a prime example of how simple fabrics can be dressed up to offer a more sophisticated look for a dining area. They are not designed to be drawn, but rather look sparkling clean and fresh while filtering the light in this sunny, all-white kitchen.

MATERIALS AND EQUIPMENT
cream linen
unbleached linen
matching sewing thread
sewing kit
curtain clips

MEASURING UP
A = width of window frame
B = length from bottom of pole
to window sill

CUTTING OUT
main panel:
width = A plus 3cm (1in)
length = B plus 3cm (1in)

short borders (cut 2):
width = 8cm (3in)
length = A plus 3cm (1in)

long borders (cut 2):
width = 8cm (3in)
length = B plus 3cm (1in)

ties (cut 7):
width = 8cm (3in)
length = 70cm (28in)

tie-top panel blind

This tie-top rectangular panel is the cheat's version of
a Roman blind, made without any rings or complicated
stringing. The pleats are held up at either side with
curtain clips; to let down the blind at night, simply
remove the clips. The ties and the narrow border are
made from the same fabric as the main blind, but in
a slightly darker shade.

1 Press under a 1.5cm (½in)
turning along one long
edge of each border strip.

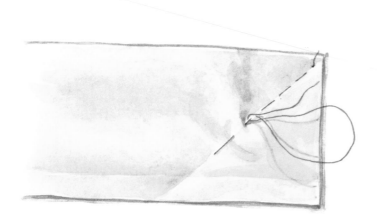

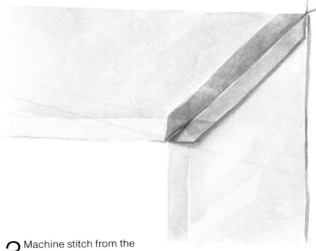

2 With right sides together and the creases matching, pin the ends of one short and one long border together. Fold the corner down to the edge opposite the crease to make a 45-degree angle and press lightly. Tack/baste along this crease with small stitches.

3 Machine stitch from the corner inwards, as far as the inner crease. Work a few extra stitches at each end to strengthen the seam. Trim the seam allowance to 1cm (½in), and press the seam open.

4 Join on the remaining strips in the same way. Lay the panel flat with the wrong side facing upwards. Place the frame over it with the right side facing downwards. Pin, tack/baste and machine stitch around the outside edge, leaving a 1.5cm (½in) seam allowance.

5 Clip and trim the corners so that they will lie flat. Turn the frame to the other side, easing the corners into shape with a knitting needle, and press.

6 Pin and tack/baste the inside edge of the frame to the panel, then machine stitch down 3mm (⅛in) from the fold. Work a round of machine stitch 3mm (⅛in) from the outside edge.

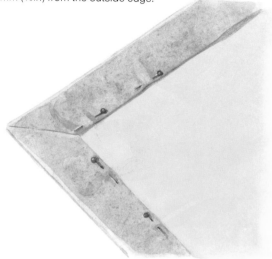

7 To make the ties, press under a 1.5cm (½in) hem along each side. Fold in half lengthways with wrong sides together and pin and tack/baste around the three open sides. Machine stitch, 3mm (⅛in) from the edge.

8 Fold the ties in half. Pin, tack/baste and machine stitch the folds to the wrong side of the panel top at regular intervals.

9 Knot the ties onto the curtain rings. Fold up into pleats and fasten them in place with curtain clips.

BEDROOMS

Bedrooms are essentially private spaces; the nearest most of us come to having a personal sanctuary. Aspirations that they be calm and restful are universal, and here, perhaps more than in any other room we are free – partners allowing – to give full rein to our personal flights of fancy, though this indulgence can lead to dangerous excesses.

Most bedrooms are relatively meanly proportioned, with the bed dominating the room and the little floor area remaining taken up with storage. For this reason, be mindful when tempted to choose a patterned fabric for curtains or blinds. When these window treatments are combined with matching bedding, a modestly sized bedroom can easily seem like a sea of fabric.

To enhance the sense of space, use a plain/solid or subtly patterned, light-coloured fabric – pale blues and greens are particularly soothing. Floor-length curtains will add height if the ceiling is low, but if space is at a premium, resist the temptation to make them heavily gathered or to allow them to puddle on the floor, as their bulk will

opposite, above left Light exclusion isn't a consideration in this all-white bedroom. Three-quarter-length voile curtains at the windows act as a pretty frame and link up with the curtain-as-headboard arrangement over the bed.

opposite, above right Lightweight, patterned curtains hung from the ceiling enwrap this cocoon-like room.

opposite, below left Gilded antique pelmets/valances lift these subdued curtains above the ordinary.

opposite, below right Discrete, space-enhancing cream Roman blinds team up with the luxury of a bed canopy and false bed hangings, adding a feeling of space to this small, but serene room.

this page It is perhaps fitting that vintage bed linen should find a new role as Roman blinds in a bedroom. Interlining the blinds renders them light-proof.

opposite Not for the faint-hearted, this cotton jungle print used for curtains, the bed and a bolster shows that bedroom soft furnishings needn't look overtly feminine. Teamed with plain walls, white bed linen and an understated carpet, the bold print is kept under control.

this page In stark contrast, these traditional-style, lined and interlined jacquard-weave curtains take a sedate role in this similarly toned interior. Sheer roller blinds allow for both light and privacy during the day.

visually and physically intrude into the room; at the very least keep them in check with tiebacks.

The degree to which light needs to be blocked out depends on the individual; some of us would probably never wake up without the rallying help of daylight, but for others every chink of light needs to be excluded. To banish sunlight, use heavy, tightly woven fabrics, line and interline lighter ones, or use special blackout cloths (which aren't necessarily black), making sure that the curtain or blind is generous enough to overlap the edges of the window frame.

A layered treatment, such as sheers teamed with a blackout blind, is especially effective in a bedroom, accommodating several different levels of privacy and light exclusion: bedrooms aren't just used for sleeping in after all, but often double up as dressing rooms, home offices and quiet spaces.

Where the bedroom does double up as a study area, avoid overtly frilly or girlie fabrics and curtain styles which won't be conducive to getting down to work. Instead, bring those elements into the room with cushions and throws that can be put away during the day.

1 Following the manufacturer's instructions and working outside or in a well-ventilated room, coat the fabric with stiffening spray. When dry, cut to size.

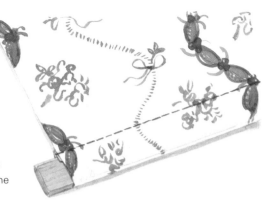

2 Press under a hem along the bottom to form a casing for the lath, then pin, tack/baste and machine stitch it down. The depth will depend on the size of the lath; check the guidelines supplied with the kit. Cut the lath to 1cm (½in) shorter than the blind and slip it into the casing.

floral roller blind

Often thought of as utilitarian and consigned to the kitchen or bathroom, roller blinds can also be attractive and versatile. This floral blind provides a useful screen for a bedroom window, whilst the bobble-trimmed voile curtains are purely decorative. Kits containing all the components – along with comprehensive instructions – for making a blind are readily available from good furnishing suppliers and department stores.

3 Cut the dowelling to size and hammer the second metal cap in place. Mark the midpoints of the rod and of the top of the fabric, then match the two together. Starting from the centre and working out towards each end, staple the fabric to the dowelling with the right side facing outwards.

MATERIALS AND EQUIPMENT
closely woven cotton fabric
stiffening spray
matching sewing thread
roller-blind kit
hacksaw, hammer and
screwdriver
staple gun
basic sewing kit

MEASURING UP AND CUTTING OUT
If blind is to hang inside a window recess:
width = width of window recess minus 2cm (¾in)
length = from top of recess to sill plus 25cm (10in)

IF BLIND IT TO HANG OUTSIDE A WINDOW RECESS OR OVER A FRAME:
width = distance between moulding
length = from top of frame to sill plus 25cm (10in)

4 Screw the fittings in place and attach the blind as directed.

ribbon embroidery

A plain white fabric with a loose square weave lends itself to extra embellishment. Here, long rows of basic running stitch have been embroidered down the length of the curtain using an assortment of coloured ribbons to create a subtle striped effect.

MATERIALS AND EQUIPMENT
narrow ribbon
scissors
open-weave curtain
sewing needle
matching sewing thread
large tapestry needle

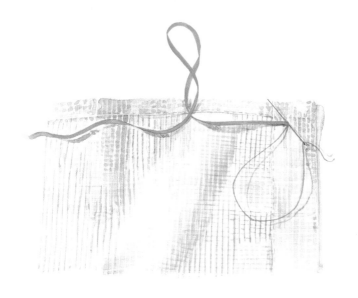

1 Cut a length of ribbon 12cm (5in) longer than the curtain and turn under 5mm (¼in) at one end. Sew the fold to the curtain just above the bottom edge, 1cm (½in) in from the side hem.

2 Thread the other end of the ribbon through a large tapestry needle. Work a row of evenly spaced running stitches about 1cm (½in) apart. Pull the ribbon up after every few stitches, keeping an even tension to prevent the fabric distorting.

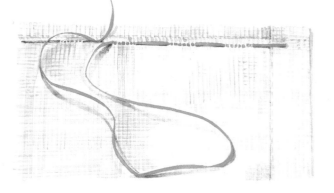

3 Continue sewing up to the top of the curtain. Trim the ribbon, fold under the end and finish off with a few stitches.

4 Embroider the rest of the curtain in the same way, alternating the colours and leaving 12cm (5in) spaces between the ribbons.

CHILDREN'S ROOMS

The main thing to bear in mind when decorating a child's room is that his or her tastes will change very rapidly as they grow up. What appeals to a toddler now is likely to be deeply, deeply uncool, just a few years down the line.

With this in mind, however tempting it is to indulge your child's (or your own) desire for pretty, pastel pinks and blues, or twee, coordinated fabrics and wallpapers featuring nursery prints or cartoon characters, ask yourself do you really want, and can you afford, to change the scheme on a regular basis?

A safer option for expensive features like curtains and blinds is to choose plain/solid or simple cheery patterned fabrics, like checks, stripes and spots in primary colours. Together with plain walls (which can easily and quickly be repainted as and when necessary), these should see children through to their teens. These sorts of fabrics have the additional benefit that they can be easily customized along the way with appliquéd panels for the curtains or themed borders for the walls.

opposite Checks and tiny flowers in navy and white would suit girls of any age, as well as younger boys. A multi-layered treatment is flexible enough to adapt to different sleeping patterns.

this page If it weren't for the presence of the rocking horse, it would be difficult to guess the age of this bedroom's owner. The use of red and white checks and pretty florals makes it child-friendly without being twee.

Children's bedrooms are the place to have fun with fabrics and furnishings. These simple cream curtains are given a groovy edge with multicoloured tassels and would easily last a child through to the teenage years, if not beyond.

Alternatively, opt for decorative schemes that appeal to children of all ages and consequently won't fall out of favour too quickly. A jaunty nautical look – easily achieved with blue and white stripes trimmed with rows of brightly coloured pennant flags – or a jungle theme would be popular with kids of all ages.

In any event, with the inevitable accumulation of clothes, books, posters, stickers and toys, a child's room will soon become subsumed by a riot of bright colours, so give in to the inevitable by installing plenty of shelving space to display toys and books, together with pin-boards for posters and artwork, and provide furnishings that will offer a neutral background to this chaos. Before long the room will be more than amply 'decorated' to the child's individual style and it will naturally evolve as their tastes and interests do.

On a practical note, especially with younger children and babies, establishing a bedtime routine will necessitate restricting daylight in the evenings

tasselled curtain

Ready-made curtains and blinds in neutral colours are widely available. This plain curtain has been customized with cotton tassels in bright primary colours to provide the perfect foil for the multicoloured chaos of a child's bedroom.

MATERIALS AND EQUIPMENT
plain curtain
set square/carpenter's square
long ruler/yardstick
coloured fine cotton yarn
thick card
large-eyed needle
basic sewing kit

1 Lay the curtain out flat, untying the cords if it has a gathered tape heading. Use a set square/carpenter's square to position the ruler/yardstick across the curtain 20cm (8in) down from the top edge.

2 Starting 10cm (4in) from the edge, mark a row of points at 10cm (4in) intervals across the curtain. Move the ruler down a further 20cm (8in) and mark a second row, this time starting 20cm (8in) from the edge. Repeat these rows down to the hem.

3 To make a tassel, wind the cotton yarn round a 10cm (4in) deep strip of card ten times. Cut another length of yarn approximately 30cm (12in). Thread one end under the strands and tie tightly.

4 Slip the loop off the card. Bind one end of the yarn around the neck of the tassel to form a rounded top. Knot the two ends together, then cut through the loop and trim the tassel.

5 Thread one end of the yarn through a large-eyed needle. Position the tassel over the a chalk mark and pass the needle through the curtain. If the curtain is lined, stitch to the main fabric only.

6 Sew the other end of the yarn through the curtain 5mm (¼in) away so that the tassel is held flat against the fabric. Knot the two ends together securely on the wrong side and clip.

7 Make one tassel for each marked point, varying the colours so they are evenly scattered across the curtain. Re-gather the curtain, if necessary, and hang.

and mornings and for afternoon naps, so children's curtains need to be ultra-efficient at blocking out the light. Line and interline curtains; if you are using a light-coloured curtain fabric consider using special blackout lining or, more flexibly, partnering the curtains with a blackout blind. Modern versions of blackout fabric aren't actually black and are specially designed to allow air to circulate through them.

Remember, too, that no matter how much thought – and money – is put into the furnishings you select, they are more than likely to be quickly vandalized with crayon and paint, irrespective of whether or not paper is to hand, so make sure that the curtain fabric can be washed and the blinds wiped.

If you think your children might have mountaineering tendencies, it would be a good idea to make curtains sill-length rather than extending them to the floor. To minimize other possible injuries, avoid hard decorative details, such as metal holdbacks and bosses, or loose lengths of fabric, such as ribbon tiebacks, which could potentially choke a child.

above A mish-mash of pretty, floral fabrics in blues and yellows looks cosy, without being cloying, while the frilly coronet above the bed would delight any aspiring princess.

left Pink may be viewed as a girlie shade, but the addition of a grown-up desk and some sophisticated pictures takes this pink and white scheme into adulthood.

this picture Essentially a plain white room, this nursery is 'decorated' for a child with the addition of sunny yellow curtains and a selection of toys.

decorative panels

Ready-made curtains can be customized with panels of patterned fabric to make them look more interesting. In this child's bedroom, two colourways of the same print have been used to upholster a low chair and to decorate the cream curtains. Each panel is edged with a different colour braid, carefully chosen to blend with the material.

MATERIALS AND EQUIPMENT
plain/solid unlined curtains
newspaper
printed fabric
woven braid in three colours
matching sewing thread
basic sewing kit

CUTTING OUT
Each curtain has two square- and one diamond-shaped panel. Cut out the shapes from newspaper and lay them out on the curtain to determine the size and layout before cutting the fabric. (Untie the gathering cords first if the curtain has a tape heading.)

1 Lay the curtain out on the floor and place the three fabric panels in position. Pin and tack/baste each one around the outside edge, ensuring the fabric remains flat.

2 Turn the end of the first length of braid under at 45 degrees and pin it to one corner of the first panel. Pin it along all four sides, mitring each corner, then tuck under the other end to neaten the join. Tack/baste in place.

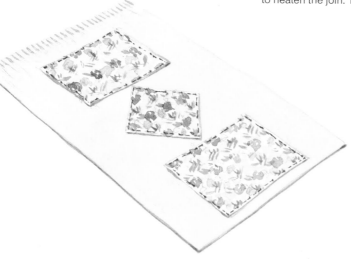

3 Machine stitch along both sides of the braid, 3mm (⅛in) in from the edge. Sew both rows in the same direction so the braid does not pucker.

4 Edge the other two panels in the same way and re-gather the heading, if necessary. Decorate the second curtain to make a matching pair.

BATHROOMS

When you consider that bathrooms are invariably steamy and damp places where hygiene is the primary concern, it's a wonder we bring fabric into them at all, but we are creatures who seek comfort and it is perhaps instinctive to wish to soften the starkness of hard surfaces like ceramic and enamel.

As there is little that we do in bathrooms that does not require the screening effects of a curtain or blind, it makes sense to have a solution that is in place all of the time, and that perhaps works equally well for the daytime and night-time. Screens featuring decorative fretwork in the Arabian style would be both practical and effective. More flexible are plantation shutters – which are similar to louvre shutters except that the slats are adjustable – and the obvious blind would be a Venetian one. They are available with either very narrow slats for a contemporary look or wider metal or wooden slats, ideal for larger windows.

For bathroom curtains, sheers are a sensible lightweight choice, but remember that electric light can render flat or lightly gathered sheer fabrics revealingly transparent at night, so unless you are prepared to use heavily gathered sheers – which will significantly reduce natural light during the day – you may have to fall back on a layered solution, say a neat roller blind teamed with lightly gathered curtains.

opposite, above left Here the window treatment in a traditional bathroom marries a practical Venetian blind with a decorative pleated blind. Using the same clean blue colour for both unites what are disparate styles.

opposite, above right It is not normally necessary to exclude light completely in a bathroom, so a semi-sheer blind is ideal, allowing some light in while preserving the modesty of the bather.

opposite, below left A London blind is a good compromise in a bathroom which could do with 'softening' a little. This unstructured style looks elegant while being easily dismantled for cleaning.

this page and opposite, below right A Venetian blind is perfect for a bathroom, being endlessly adjustable to suit every requirement. By matching the colour to the décor it blends into the architecture.

Bathrooms, like kitchens, may be the place to break with the aesthetic rule that states curtains look better floor length. Sill-length curtains will prevent fabric from routinely sitting in wet puddles on the floor and may, in any event, be the only option where the basin or bath has been placed under the window.

Fabrics, if they are not to end up looking like limp rags, should be robust enough to withstand the inevitable steam. Stout linen, tightly woven cotton or a plasticized fabric will do the job. Or, employing some lateral thinking, what about oilcloth or shower curtain fabric, which by necessity has to be waterproof, damp-proof and rot-proof?

Other unusual solutions include variations on the beaded curtain. Consider making one using a variety of glass or plastic beads instead of the more traditional wooden type. Rust-resistant metal chain or lengths of ribbon weighted down with pretty objects are other interesting alternatives. Whatever solution you come up with, enlist a friend to verify that the window treatment is really as successful as you believe it to be!

above This over-length pewter-coloured sheer makes a glamorous statement in a bathroom designed for luxurious relaxation. But note that such a fine fabric will only provide privacy during the day!

right A vintage Paco Rabanne dress of metal discs has been transformed into a curtain suspended from a sliding track. It provides privacy from the outside while allowing glimpses of the view for bathers looking out.

ribbon and shell curtains

This alternative to the traditional bead curtain is an original way to display the results of a day's beachcombing. The shells are tied to translucent ribbons and hung from a bamboo pole. Search for scallops, clams and limpets that have been worn by the sea, or hunt out abalones and other shells with natural holes.

MATERIALS AND EQUIPMENT
selection of ribbons in various widths
scissors
shells
bamboo cane the width of the window
bradawl/awl
2 cup hooks

1 Cut a piece of ribbon to length, allowing an extra 15cm (6in) for the two knots. Choose a shell with a natural hole in it and thread one end of the ribbon through and tie tightly. Wrap the other end once around the cane 2cm (¾in) in from the end and knot in place.

2 Use a longer ribbon to tie round a shell without a hole, wrapping it widthways and then lengthways. Finish off with a knot at the shortest edge.

3 Tie the remaining shells along the pole, varying the lengths and colours of the ribbons and leaving a 2cm (¾in) space at the other end.

4 Make a hole either side of the window frame using a bradawl/awl and screw in the cup hooks. Slip the cane into the hooks to hang the curtain.

PRACTICALITIES

BASIC SEWING KIT

The equipment and techniques needed for the projects in this book are minimal, but it is worth investing in the best possible tools.

Sewing machine

Modern sewing machines have many advanced stitching features, but most curtains need only a basic straight stitch and a zigzag for neatening seams/finishing raw edges. Always use a sharp needle and match its thickness to the weight of the fabric. The finest needles have the lowest numbers, so use size 8 for sheers, 12 for most projects and a size 16 for heavy canvas.

Scissors

Dressmaking shears with long blades are used for cutting out and should be kept well sharpened. The handles are bent at an angle so that they can cut accurately.
Sewing scissors are smaller and have straight handles. Use these for trimming seams and clipping corners.
Embroidery scissors have short, pointed blades, which make them ideal for trimming thread and notching seam allowances.
Paper scissors should be kept specially for cutting out patterns and templates.

Needles

Hand-sewing needles come in various sizes for different tasks. Medium-length sharps are best for general sewing and tacking/basting, and shorter betweens can be used for slip stitch. Crewel needles have an extra-long eye designed for embroidery threads.

Thimble

A flat-top metal thimble should be used to protect the fingers when tacking/basting heavy fabrics together, but it may take a while to get used to.

Dressmaker's pins

These can be used for fine fabrics; larger glass-headed pins show up better on thicker material. Check that they are made from rustless steel.

Sewing thread

Always choose a thread made from the same weight and fibre as the fabric being stitched. Mercerized cotton has a smooth surface and should be used for stitching cotton and linens. Polyester thread is finer and can be used for mixed fabrics. Match the colour as closely as possible, and choose a darker shade if an exact match is not possible.

Tacking/basting thread

The loosely spun thread used for tacking/basting is not mercerized, which means it breaks easily and can be unpicked without damaging a finished seam. Use a contrasting colour that shows up well when tacking/basting stitches are being removed.

Marking tools

Tailor's chalk, which comes in a thin, solid block, produces a fine line that brushes away easily. Use white for dark fabrics and the coloured versions to mark paler cloth.
Chalk pencils can be sharpened to a fine point for detailed marking.

Dressmaker's pens have a water-soluble or light-sensitive ink that washes out or fades completely a few hours after use without leaving any marks.

Iron

Hems and seams must be pressed well, so you need a good steam iron and a large ironing board. Use a cleaning cloth to remove any build-up.

Measurements

Precise measurement is vital, so obtain a good tape measure that will not stretch with use and become inaccurate.

CURTAIN FITTINGS

Poles, rods and tracks contribute as much to the finished look of a window treatment as the curtains themselves; the two should complement each other, so spend as much time choosing the fittings as you do on the design and the fabric.

Wood and metal poles are a decorative feature in themselves, often with ornate ends or finials, and are available in every style from a minimalist iron rod to baroque and classical reproductions. They are mounted on brackets screwed to the wall above the window. A heavy curtain will need a strong support, whilst lightweight sheers can be hung from a simple sprung rod, tension wire or a length of curtain wire on cuphooks.

Tracks are concealed when the curtains are drawn together, and are often covered up with a pelmet/valance when the curtains are open. Some have a pull-cord system so the curtains can be opened and closed without handling them directly – this is ideal for delicate fabrics that can easily be damaged. Metal tracks should be used for thicker fabrics and flexible tracks can be fitted to curved bay windows.

MEASURING A WINDOW FOR CURTAINS

The curtain fitting should be in place before you start to measure. Allow sufficient overlap at each side of the window for the curtain to be pulled back: heavy curtains will require more wall space than sheers so that they do not block too much light. Check that there is room for any tie- or holdbacks: you should position these once the curtains have been hung.

Width [A]

For each curtain, take your measurement from the centre of the window to the end of the pole, excluding the finial. If the track is made in two parts, allow 10cm (4in) or more extra for the overlap. Some metal fittings have an angled return at each end, creating a corner to accommodate the fabric when the curtains are drawn right back; add on this length if necessary.

Length [B]

For full-length curtains, measure from the top of the track or the bottom of the rings to the floor. If you want a look that spills onto the floor, add an extra 50cm (10in) or more to the finished length. Short curtains are measured to just below the sill, or to sill length if the window is deeply recessed.

CUTTING OUT FABRIC

Press the fabric to remove any creases and lay it out flat before cutting to the correct size. A large dining table is ideal, but a clean floor will work just as well. Cut off the selvedges or snip into them at 10cm (4in) intervals (the edges of the fabric are often woven tightly and will distort the seams so that the curtain will not drape properly).

Use a set square/carpenter's square and a long ruler/yardstick to mark the horizontal cutting lines at right angles to the sides. If your fabric has a loose weave, you may be able to pull out a weft thread across the width to mark the line. Label the top edge of each piece: even plain/solid fabrics may have variations in the weave that will reflect the light differently.

JOINING FABRIC WIDTHS

A centre seam can look awkward – particularly on a blind – so if the panel has two drops cut one of them in half. Sew the two narrow pieces to the outside edges.

JOINING FABRIC WIDTHS

WORKING WITH PATTERNED FABRICS

Any fabrics with a pattern – from small scale checks to floral prints – must be matched up when two or more drops are joined to create the required width, and also across both curtains to make a pair. Measure the depth of the pattern repeat and add this onto each length when calculating the amount of fabric needed. When cutting out the panels, ensure that the top edge of each drop starts at the same point on the design.

The lengths should be joined so the design matches horizontally across the seam line. Press under the seam allowance on the first length and place it over the second, adjusting it so that the patterns match exactly. Pin close to the fold, then tack/baste the seam allowances together on the wrong side. Machine stitch along the crease line.

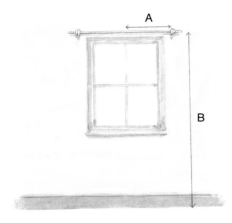

MEASURING UP A WINDOW FOR CURTAINS

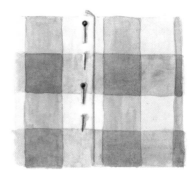

JOINING PATTERNED FABRIC

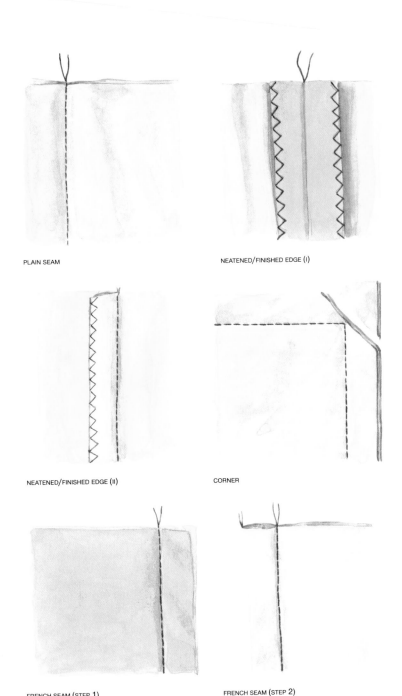

PLAIN SEAM

NEATENED/FINISHED EDGE (I)

NEATENED/FINISHED EDGE (II)

CORNER

FRENCH SEAM (STEP 1)

FRENCH SEAM (STEP 2)

SEAMS

The extra fabric needed to join two pieces of fabric is given as the seam allowance. To keep it consistent, match the raw edges to the corresponding line on the bed of the sewing machine when stitching.

Plain seam

Line up the two raw edges with right sides together. Pin together at intervals of 5 to 10cm (2 to 4in), inserting the pins at right angles to the fabric or parallel to the edge. Tack/baste, then machine stitch along the seam line. Press the seam open or to one side as directed and unpick the tacking/basting.

Neatened/finished edge

The cut edge of a plain seam may fray, especially if an item is washed. To prevent this, a line of zigzag or overlock stitch can be worked along each raw edge before seaming if the seam is to be pressed open (i). If the seam is to be pressed to one side, the seam allowance can be trimmed and the two edges joined together with a zigzag (ii).

Corner

To sew round a right-angled corner, stitch to the end of the seam allowance. Lift the presser foot, leaving the needle down. Turn the fabric through 90 degrees, and continue stitching. Clip off the corner to within 2mm (⅟₁₆ in) of the stitching before turning through, so that it will lie flat.

French seam

Used for joining lightweight or sheer fabrics, this seam encloses the raw edges on the wrong side. With wrong sides together, seam the fabric 8mm (⅜ in) from the edge. Trim the allowance to 6mm (¼ in) and fold the right sides together. Stitch again, 8mm (⅜ in) from the edge.

HEMS

The finish to the lower edge of a piece of fabric depends on its weight.

Single hem

Used for heavier linens and upholstery fabrics. Zigzag the raw edge and press the turning up to the required length on the wrong side. Pin and tack/baste, then sew in place by hand or machine stitch just below the zigzag.

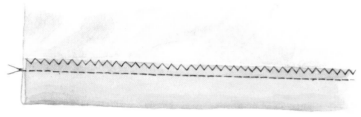

SINGLE HEM

Double hem

Consists of one narrow and one deeper turning or two equal turnings, which give a firmer edge to finer fabrics. Press under 6mm (¼in) along the raw edge, then turn up to length as directed. Pin and tack/baste, then either machine stitch close to the inner fold or finish by hand for a neater result.

DOUBLE HEM

HAND STITCHING

The majority of the sewing for all the projects in this book is stitched by machine, but hand sewing is vital for tacking/basting and finishing off hems, mitres and some seams.

Slip stitch

Used to join two folded edges or to secure a folded hem. Bring the needle out through the fold and pick up two threads of the other fabric. Pass the needle back through the fold for 6mm (¼in) and repeat to the end.

SLIP STITCH

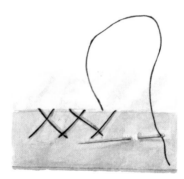

HERRINGBONE STITCH

Herringbone stitch

Creates a flat, unobtrusive hem for curtains. Bring the needle up inside the hem and make a diagonal stitch up to the right, then a short horizontal stitch to the left. Work a diagonal stitch down to the right and, taking the needle through the top layer of the hem, make a short horizontal stitch to the left. Repeat these two stitches to continue.

RESOURCES

UK

Alison White
+ 44 (0)20 8351 0001
www.alisonwhite.co.uk
*Understated magnetic blinds
and modular screens.*

The Blue Door
77 Church Road
London SW13 0DQ
+ 44 (0)20 8748 9785
www.bluedoorbarnes.co.uk
*Custom-made Swedish and
rolled blinds, plus kits for DIY
Swedish blinds.*

The Bradley Collection
Lion Barn
Maitland Road
Needham Market
Suffolk IP6 8NS
+ 44 (0)845 118 7224
www.bradleycollection.co.uk
*Manufacturers of modern
metal poles and finials.*

The Button Queen
19 Marylebone Lane
London W1M 2NF
+ 44 (0)20 7935 1505
www.thebuttonqueen.co.uk
*Period and contemporary
buttons in every style.*

The Cane Store
Washdyke Cottage
1 Witham Road
Long Bennington
Newark
Lincs NG23 5DS
+ (0)1400 282271
www.canestore.co.uk
Bamboo poles and blinds.

Cath Kidston
+ 44 (0)20 7221 4000
www.cathkidston.co.uk
*Vintage florals and prints in
contemporary style; curtains
and blinds made to measure.*

Colefax and Fowler
110 Fulham Road
London SW3 6HU
+ 44 (0)20 7244 7427
www.colefax.com
Classic, timeless fabrics.

Creative Beadcraft
20 Beak Street
London W1F 9RE
+44 (0)20 7629 9964
www.creativebeadcraft.co.uk
*An amazing selection of
glass, bone, wood and
plastic beads.*

Designers Guild
267 & 277 Kings Road
London SW3 5UH
+ 44 (0) 7351 5775
www.designersguild.com
*Furnishing fabrics from
over 50 collections.*

Eclectics
+ 44 (0)1843 852888
www.eclectics.co.uk
*Made-to-measure
contemporary blinds
featuring an extensive range
of styles and materials.*

The Final Curtain Company
+ 44 (0)20 8699 3626
finalcurtaincompany.com
*Curtains and blinds made
to measure from natural
silks and cottons.*

Faber Blinds
Kilvey Road
Brackmills
Northampton NN4 7PB
+ 44 (0)1604 766251
www.faberblinds.co.uk
*Ready-made and made-to-
measure vertical, Venetian
and roller blinds.*

Great English Outdoors
Castle Street
Hay-on-Wye
Herefordshire HR3 5DF
+ 44 (0)1497 821205
www.greatenglish.co.uk
*Hundreds of vintage Welsh
blankets waiting to be
transformed into curtains.*

Ian Mankin
109 Regent's Park Road
London NW1 8UR
+ 44 (0)20 7722 0997
www.ianmankin.com
Tickings and utility fabrics.

Ikea
+ 44 (0)20 8208 5600
www.ikea.co.uk
*A wide range of soft
furnishings.*

John Lewis
+ 44 (0)20 7828 100
www.johnlewis.com
*Department store with more
than 25 branches nationwide.*

Kleins
5 Noel Street
London W1F 8GD
+ 44 (0)20 7437 6162
www.kleins.co.uk
Specialist haberdasher.

Luxaflex
+ 44 (0)800 652 7769
www.luxaflex.com
Innovative blinds.

MacCulloch & Wallis
25–26 Dering Street
London W1S 1AT
+ 44 (0)20 7629 0311
www.macculloch-wallis.co.uk
*Affordable ribbons, braids,
trimmings and fashion
accessories as well as fabrics
and sewing equipment.*

Malabar
31–33 The South Bank
Business Centre
Ponton Road
London SW8 5BL
+ 44 (0)20 7501 4200
www.malabar.co.uk
*Brightly coloured, mainly
handloom fabrics including
cotton voiles and silks.*

McKinney & Co
Studio P
The Old Imperial Laundry
71 Warriner Gardens
London SW11 4XW
+ 44 (0)20 7627 5077
www.mckinney.co.uk
*An amazing range of finials,
poles, pelmets and tiebacks.*

The Natural Fabric Company
Dovedale Farmhouse
Blockley, Moreton-in-Marsh
Gloucestershire GL56 9TS
+ 44 (0)1386 700900
www.naturalfabric
company.com
*Toile de Jouy, cottons,
ginghams and linens, voiles
and silk, crewel work, ticking
and hessian – all natural.*

New House Textiles
How Caple Court
How Caple
Herefordshire HR1 4SX
+ 44 (0)1989 740684
www.newhousetextiles.co.uk
*Roman blinds, vertical blinds,
pulls, weights and tiebacks.*

Pax Mariae
35 Walcot Street
Bath BA1 5BN
01225 480660
*Fabrics in traditional and
modern Swedish patterns;
handmade glass rings for
making up Swedish blinds.*

Texture
84 Stoke Newington
Church Street
London N16 0AP
+ 44 (0)20 7241 0990
*Eco-friendly fabrics in
largely natural shades.*

VV Rouleaux
102 Marylebone Lane
London W1U 2QD
+ 44 (0)20 7224 5179
www.vvrouleaux.com
*Vast selection of ribbons,
braids, trims, flowers, tassels
and tiebacks.*

Walcot House
Lyneham Heath Studios
Lyneham, Chipping Norton
Oxfordshire OX7 6QQ
+ 44 (0)1993 832940
www.walcothouse.com
Poles and accessories.

Warris Vianni & Co
85 Golborne Road
London W10 5NL
020 8964 0069
www.warrisvianni.com
*Beautiful fabrics in natural
fibres sourced from artisans
and weavers all over India.*

Wendy Cushing Passementerie
2/11 Chelsea Harbour
Design Centre
London SW10 0XE
+ 44 (0)20 7352 6323
www.wendycushing.com
*Traditional and contemporary
trimmings including tassels,
braid and fringes.*

Whaleys
Harris Court
Great Horton
Bradford
West Yorkshire BD7 4EQ
+ 44 (0)1274 576718
www.whaleys-bradford.ltd.uk
*Vast range of natural fabrics
such as cotton duck, linen,
canvas, twill and hessian.*

USA

ABC Carpet & Home
888 Broadway
New York, NY 10003
+ 1 212 473 3000
www.abchome.com
*Fabrics, furniture and other
home products.*

A. C. Moore
+ 1 866 342 8802
www.acmoore.com
*Craft superstore with over
70 branches.*

All State Glass Corp.
85 Kenmare Street
New York, NY 10012
+ 1 212 226 2517
www.allstateglasscorp.com
Blinds and shutters.

B & J Fabrics
263 West 40th Street
New York, NY 10018
+ 1 212 354 8150
*Natural-fibre fabrics. Search
and special-order services.*

Ballard Designs
1670 Defoor Avenue, NW
Atlanta, GA 30318
800 367 2775
www.ballarddesigns.com
Furniture, fabrics; custom workroom.

Baranzelli Home
1127 Second Avenue
New York, NY 10022
212 753 6511
High-quality fabrics and trimmings.

Bechenstein's Home Fabrics
4 West 20th Street
New York, NY 10011
+ 1 212 366 5142
A wide choice of fabrics.

Bed Bath & Beyond
620 Avenue of the Americas
New York, NY 10011
+ 1 212 255 3550
Home superstore, including window treatments.

Bloomingdales
1000 Third Avenue
New York, NY 10022
+ 1 212 705 2000
www.bloomingdales.com
Department stores with decorating departments.

Calico Corners
+ 1 800 213 6366
www.calicocorners.com
Fabric from manufacturers such as Waverly, Ralph Lauren. Many stores nationwide.

Clotilde, Inc.
B 3000
Louisiana, MO 63353
+ 1 800 772 2891
www.clotilde.com
Discounted notions, trims and threads.

C. M. Offray & Sons, Inc.
Route 24
P. O. Box 601
Chester, NJ 07930
+ 1 908 879 4700
www.offray.com
Woven and wire-edge ribbons, flowers, and bows. From fabric and notion stores nationwide.

Country Curtains
The Red Lion Inn
Stockbridge, MA 01262
+ 1 413 298 5565
+ 1 800 876 6123
www.countrycurtains.com
Fabric and lace curtains, swags, hardware and accessories.

Cowtan & Tout, Inc.
979 Third Avenue
New York, NY 10022
+ 1 212 753 4488
Traditional fabrics to trade, from silk brocades to prints on linen.

Crate and Barrel
+ 1 800 967 6696
www.crateandbarrel.com
Home accessories for contemporary living.

The Fabric Center
485 Electric Avenue
Fitchburg, MA 01420
+ 1 978 343 4402
Discounted decorator fabrics.

French General
35 Crosby Street
New York, NY 10012
+ 1 212 343 7474
frenchgeneral.com
Vintage notions, ribbon, velvet leaves and flowers, glass garlands, and decor items from French flea markets.

Hancock Fabrics
+ 1 662 844 7368
www.hancockfabrics.com
Everything you need for projects involving sewing or fabrics.

Harry Zarin
292 Grand Street
New York, NY 10002
+ 1 212 925 6112
www.harryzarin.com
Large selection of discounted fabrics and blinds.

Home Depot
www.homedepot.com
Everything for the home.

Ikea
www.ikea.com
A large range of home furnishings.

Inter-Coastal Textile
480 Broadway
New York, NY 10013
Decorative fabrics at a discount.

Jo-Ann
+ 1 800 525 4951
www.joann.com
Craft supplies for all projects.

Keepsake Quilting
Route 25B
P.O. Box 1618
Center Harbor, NH 03226-1618
+ 1 800 865 9458
www.keepsakequilting.com
Lightweight cottons and a wide range of threads and notions.

K. Trimming Co.
519 Broadway
New York, NY 10012
+ 1 212 431 8929
Incredible collection of notions and trimmings.

Laura Ashley, Inc.
+ 1 800 553 5309
www.lauraashley-usa.com
Cotton fabrics with English garden look.

Levolor Home Fashions
309 N. Prospect Street
Sturgis, MI 49091
+ 1 800 528 1407
www.levolor.com
Blinds, hardware and rods.

Lowe's
+ 1 800 445 6937
www.lowes.com
More than 1,500 home improvement stores nationwide.

Macy's
+ 1 800 BUY-MACY
www.macys.com
Department stores nationwide.

Metropolitan Impex
966 Avenue of the Americas
New York, NY 10018
+ 1 212 502 5243
www.metropolitanimpex.com
Good selection of trimmings, feathers, laces and beads.

Michaels
+ 1 800 642 4235
www.michaels.com
Speciality retailer of arts and crafts items.

Nancy's Notions
P.O. Box 683
Beaver Dam, WI 53916
+ 1 800 833 0690
www.nancysnotions.com
Notions, trims, threads, books and videos for the home sewer.

Nieman Marcus
+ 1 800 825 8000
www.neimanmarcus.com
Department stores and catalog.

Oppenheim's
P.O. Box 29
120 East Main Street
North Manchester
IN 46962-0052
+ 1 800 461 6728
Country prints, chambray, denim, flannel fabrics, and mill remnants.

Pauline Yeats
26 East 22nd Street
New York, NY 10003
+ 1 212 228 5353
Designer furniture and fabrics.

Penn & Fletcher
21-07 41st Avenue, 5th Floor
New York, NY 11101
+ 1 212 239 6868
www.pennandfletcher.com
Quality trims and lace, beading and embroidery.

Pierre Deux
+ 1 888 743 7732
www.pierredeux.com
French printed fabrics. Custom drapery service. Unique trims.

Pottery Barn
+ 1 888 779 5176
www.potterybarn.com
Furniture and accessories. Stores nationwide.

Quinns Essentials
19 East Cross Street
Ypsilanti, MI 48198
+ 1 734 544 4690
+ 1 877 7 QUINNS
www.quinnsessentials.com
Large selection of name-brand fabrics. Interior design studio.

Renovators Supply
San Francisco, CA 94117
+ 1 415 563 2727
Drapery hardware.

Rose Brand
75 Ninth Avenue, 4th Floor
New York, NY 10011
+ 1 212 242 7554
www.rosebrand.com
Theatrical fabrics, custom draperies, muslins, wide widths, sheers, netting and trimmings.

Rue de France
78 Thomas Street
Newport, RI 02840
401 846 3636
+ 1 800 777 0998
www.ruedefrance.com
All types of hardware and a selection of fabric curtains and accessories.

Silk Trading Co.
360 South La Brea Avenue
Los Angeles, CA 90036
+ 1 800 854 0396
www.silktrading.com
More than 2,000 silk fabrics, from taffeta to classic damask, ready-made curtains, trimmings, lampshades.

Smith & Noble
P.O. Box 1387
Corona, CA 91718
+ 1 800 560 0027
www.smithandnoble.com
All kinds of blinds and window treatments.

Sundial & Schwartz
159 East 118th Street
New York, NY 10035
+ 1 212 289 4969
www.sundial.baweb.com
Blinds and other window treatments.

Thai Silks!
252 State Street
Los Altos, CA 94022
+ 1 800 722 7455
www.thaisilks.com
Silk, velvet, organza, jacquard, taffeta.

West Elm
+ 1 888 922 4119
www.westelm.com
Modern home accessories in a zenlike style.

BUSINESS CREDITS
ARCHITECTS AND DESIGNERS WHOSE WORK IS FEATURED IN THIS BOOK

**Andrew Arnott and
Karin Shack**
Art & Design
517 High Street, Prahran
Victoria 3181
Australia
Page 17r.

Andrew Parr
SJB Interior Design Pty Ltd
Studio Southbank
5 Haig Street
South Melbourne 3205
Australia
Page 51b.

Ash Sakula Architects
24 Rosebery Avenue
London EC1R 4SX
UK
+ 44 (0)7837 9735
info@ashsak.com
www.ashsak.com
Page 57r.

Azman Associates
(formerly Azman Owens
Architects)
10 Charlotte Road
London EC2A 3PB
UK
+ 44 (0)7739 8191
Page 4.

Blakes Lodging
77 Pantigo Road
East Hampton
New York, NY 11937
USA
+ 1 631 324 1815
www.blakesbb.com
www.picket.com
Pages 40b, 94.

Bruno & Hélène Lafforgue
Mas de l'Ange
Maison d'Hôte
Petite route de St. Remy-de-
Provence
13946 Mollégès
France
Page 41ar.

Campion A. Platt
152 Madison Avenue
Suite 900
New York, NY 10016–5424
USA
www.campionplatt.com
Pages 28–29.

Carden Cunietti
1a Adpar Street
London W2 1DE
UK
+ 44 (0)7724 9679
cc@carden-cunietti.com
www.carden-cunietti.com
*Pages 7l, 10bl, 11, 22ar, 32, 75,
80, 106–107, 109, 130ar, 130bl,
132l, 138, endpapers.*

Charles Rutherfoord
51 The Chase
London SW4 0NP
UK
+ 44 (0)7627 0182
www.charlesrutherfoord.net
Page 62.

Charlotte Crosland Interiors
Pall Mall Deposit, Unite 19
124–28 Barlby Road
London W10 6BL
UK
+ 44 (0)8960 9442
mail@charlottecrosland.com
www.charlottecrosland.com
*Pages 2, 7c, 17c, 96–97, 98,
98–99, 99a, 105b, 110, 111,
118br, 119.*

**Christian de Falbe Interior
Design**
The Glasshouse
49a Goldhawk Road
London W12 8QP
UK
+ 44 (0)8743 3210
studio@cdef.co.uk
www.cdef.co.uk
*Pages 10ar, 21ac, 21b, 26,
27, 74all, 87a.*

Christophe Gollut
Alistair Colvin Ltd
116 Fulham Road
London SW3 6HU
UK
www.christophegollut.com
Pages 21ar, 50r.

CR Studio Architects, PC
6 West 18th Street
9th Floor
New York, NY 10011
USA
+ 1 212 989 8187
victoria@crstudio.com
www.crstudio.com
Page 118ar.

Daniel Jasiak
Designer
12 rue Jean Ferrandi
Paris 75006
France
+ 33 1 45 49 13 56
www.daniel-jasiak.com
Page 14l.

Enrica Stabile
Antiques dealer, interior
decorator & photographic stylist
L'Utile e il Dilettevole
Via Carlo Maria Maggi 6
20154 Milano
Italy
+ 39 02 34 53 60 86
www.enricastabile.com
Pages 58al, 112ar, 128a.

Eric De Queker
DQ Design In Motion
Koninklijkelaan 44
2600 Bercham
Belgium
Pages 24bl, 30br.

Fiil & Co
Designers of curtain panels and
home interiors & accessories
amfiil@c.dk
Shop:
Lavender Hill
Østergade 24B
1100 Copenhagen K
Denmark
+ 45 33 121201
*Pages 8–9, 10br, 42r both, 68br,
69 main, 69 inset left, 70–71.*

Frédéric Méchiche
4 rue de Thorigny
75003 Paris
France
Pages 41br, 86al, 86bl.

Géraldine Prieur
Interior Designer
2 Boulevard Pershing
75017 Paris
France
+ 33 6 11 19 42 86
www.geraldineprieur.com
Page 15.

Gloss Ltd
Designers of home accessories
274 Portobello Road
London W10 5TE
UK
+ 44 (0)8960 4146
pascale@glossltd.u-net.com
Page 78bl.

Hotel Villa Gallici
Aix en Provence
France
www.villagallici.com
Pages 59, 61.

Interni Pty Ltd
Interior Design Consultancy
98 Barcom Ave
Rushcutters Bay
NSW 2011
Australia
Page 51a.

IPL Interiors
25 Bullen Street
London SW11 3ER
UK
+ 44 (0)7978 4224
ipl.interiors@virgin.net
*Pages 17l, 36–39, 91ar, 120,
121, 124, 130br, 131.*

Jacomini Interior Design
1701 Brun
Suite 101
Houston, TX 77019
USA
www.jacominidesign.com
Pages 40a, 70.

James Biber, AIA
Pentagram Architecture
204 Fifth Avenue
New York, New York 10010
USA
Page 30bl.

Janie Jackson
Stylist/Designer
Parma Lilac
Children's nursery furnishings
& accessories
+ 44 (0)8960 9239
Page 24ar.

Jeff McKay Inc.
Advertising and Public
Relations Agency
203 Lafayette Street
New York, NY 10012
USA
+ 1 212 771 1770
Page 132r.

Johanne Riss
Stylist, designer & fashion
designer
35 Place du Nouveau
Marché aux Graens
1000 Brussels
Belgium
+ 32 2 513 0900
www.johanneriss.com
Page 67br.

Johnson Naylor
13 Britton Street
London EC1M 5SX
+ 44 (0)7490 8885
brian.johnson@johnson
naylor.co.uk
www.johnsonnaylor.co.uk
Page 67ar.

Kelly Hoppen Interiors
2 Alma Studios
32 Stratford Road
Kensington
London W8 6QF
UK
Page 29.

Khai Liew Design
166 Magill Road
Norwood
South Australia 5067
Australia
www.khailiewdesign.com
Page 91al.

Larcombe & Solomon
Architects
Level 3, 397 Riley Street
Surry Hills 2010
NSW
Australia
www.lsarchitects.com.au
Page 63bc.

Laura Bohn Design Associates
30 West 26th Street
11th Floor
New York, NY 10010
USA
+ 1 212 645 3636
www.laurabohndesign.com
Page 14r.

Lena Proudlock
www.lenaproudlock.com
Page 63bl.

Malin Iovino Design
+ 44 (0)7252 3542
iovino@btinternet.com
Page 112l.

Marisa Tadiotto Cavalli
Via Solferino 11
20121 Milano
Italy
+ 39 03 48 41 01 738/
+ 39 02 86 46 24 26
marisscavalli@hotmail.com
Pages 22al, 23, 68ar.

Mark Guard Architects
161 Whitfield Street
UK
London W1P 5RY
+ 44 (0)7380 1199
www.markguard.co.uk
Page 25.

Mary Drysdale
1733 Connecticut Avenue NW
Washington DC 20009
USA
Page 35.

Mullman Seidman Architects
Architecture & interior design
443 Greenwich Street, # 2A
New York, NY 10013
USA
+ 1 212 431 0770
msa@mullmanseidman.com
www.mullmanseidman.com
Page 65.

Nancy Braithwaite Interiors
2300 Peachtree Road
Suite C101
Atlanta, Georgia 30309
USA
Pages 5, 83bl, 115, 130al.

Nicholas Arbuthnott
Arbuthnott Ladenbury
Architects
15 Gosditch Street
Cirencester GL7 2AG
UK
Vanessa Arbuthnott Fabrics
The Tallet
Calmsden
Cirencester GL7 5ET
UK
www.vanessaarbuthnott.co.uk
Country House Walks Ltd
Self-catering accommodation/
weekend breaks
The Tallet
Calmsden
Cirencester GL7 5ET
UK
www.thetallet.co.uk
Page 16r.

Nicoletta Marazza
Via G Morone, 8
20121 Milan
Italy
+ 39 2 7601 4482
Page 101l.

Ogawa/Depardon Architects
69 Mercer Street, 2nd Floor
New York, NY 10012
USA
+ 1 212 627 7390
www.oda-ny.com
Page 81.

OKA Direct
Mail-order furniture and home
accessories,including rattan,
painted furniture, leather and
horn. For a catalogue, call
+ 44 (0)870 160 6002
www.okadirect.com
Page 21al.

Roger Oates Design
Shop & Showroom:
1 Munro Terrace
off Cheyne Walk
London SW10 0DL
UK
(cont. next column)

Studio Shop:
The Long Barn
Eastnor, Ledbury
Herefordshire HR8 1EL
UK
Rugs and Runners Mail Order
Catalogue:
+ 44 (0)1531 631611
www.rogeroates.co.uk
Page 101br.

Russell Glover
Architect
russellglover@earthlink.net
Page 75acr.

Sabina Fay Braxton
Cloth of Gold
Grennan Watermill
Thomastown
Co Kilkenny
Ireland
+ 353 565 4383
by appointment in New York:
+ 1 212 535 2587
by appointment in Paris:
+ 33 1 46 57 11 62
cofgold@indigo.ie
Pages 12br, 20 both, 67cr.

Sasha Waddell
www.sashawaddell.co.uk
+ 44 (0)8979 9189
Pages 13, 31b, 122.

Sequana
64 Avenue de la Motte Picquet
75015 Paris
France
+ 33 1 45 66 58 40
sequana@wanadoo.fr
Page 57bl.

Sheila Scholes
Designer
+ 44 (0)1480 498241
*Pages 6, 48, 71, 83al, 84, 85,
92, 100, 140, 144.*

Sian Colley Soft Furnishings
Block E, 2B Upper Ringway
Bounds Green
London N11 2UD
UK
+ 44 (0)8368 4092
colleysian@hotmail.com
*Pages 12a, 12bl, 56, 88, 99c,
99b, 101cr, 104–105, 105a, 113.*

Steven Roxburghe Designs
48 Kensington Church Street
London W8 4DA
UK
0845 2600 256
www.steven.roxburghe-
designs.com
Pages 28, 33all, 143.

Studio Reed
(formerly Reed Creative
Services Ltd)
151a Sydney Street
London SW3 6NT
UK
+ 44 (0)7565 0066
Page 50al.

Todhunter Earle Interiors
Interior design company based
in Chelsea; undertakes a wide
variety of projects.
Chelsea Reach, 1st Floor
79–89 Lots Road
London SW10 0RN
UK
+ 44 (0)7349 9999
interiors@todhunterearle.com
www.todhunterearle.com
*Pages 1, 52, 53, 55, 83ar,
87b, 118bl, 125, 128bl.*

Vicente Wolf Associates, Inc.
333 West 39th Street
New York, NY 10018
USA
www.vicentewolf.com
Page 101ar.

Vincent Dané
Interior Design Antiques
50 Cranby Gardens
London SW7 3DE
UK
Pages 34, 63br, 112br.

Wendy Harrop
Interior Designer
11 Rectory Road
London SW13 0DU
UK
Pages 41al, 42al.

Yves Halard
Interior Decoration
27 Quai de la Tournelle
75005 Paris
France
+ 33 1 4407 14 00
Pages 63a

PICTURE CREDITS

All illustrations by Lizzie Sanders, all photographs by Polly Eltes unless specified otherwise.

Key: ph=photographer, a=above, b=below, c=centre, l=left, r=right.

Endpapers Debby & Jeremy Amias' house in London designed by Carden Cunietti; 1 Emily Todhunter's house in London designed by Todhunter Earle Interiors; 2 A house in London designed by Charlotte Crosland Interiors; 4 ph Andrew Wood/Guido Palau's house in North London, designed by Azman Owens Architects; 5 ph Simon Upton; 6 Sheila Scholes' house near Cambridge; 7l Debby & Jeremy Amias' house in London designed by Carden Cunietti; 7c A house in London designed by Charlotte Crosland Interiors; 7r ph James Merrell/Sue and Andy A'Court; 8–9 Anne-Mette Fiil's house near Cambridge; 10al ph James Merrell/fabric from Ian Mankin; 10ar Christian de Falbe's London home; 10bl Debby & Jeremy Amias' house in London designed by Carden Cunietti; 10br Anne-Mette Fiil's house near Cambridge; 11 Debby & Jeremy Amias' house in London designed by Carden Cunietti; 12a&bl Curtain design by Sian and Annie Colley; 12br ph David Montgomery/Sabina Fay Braxton's apartment in Paris; 13 ph David Montgomery/Sasha Waddell's house in London; 14l ph Polly Wreford/Daniel Jasiak's apartment in Paris; 14r ph David Montgomery/Laura Bohn's apartment in New York designed by Laura Bohn Design Associates; 15 ph Alan Williams/Géraldine Prieur's apartment in Paris, an Interior Designer fascinated with colour; 16l ph James Merrell/fabrics from Ian Mankin, trimmings from V. V. Rouleaux; 16r ph Alan Williams/The Arbuthnott family's house near Cirencester designed by Nicholas Arbuthnott, fabrics designed by Vanessa Arbuthnott; 17l James Merrell/an apartment in London (designed by François Gilles & Dominique Lubar, IPL Interiors); 17c A house in London designed by Charlotte Crosland Interiors; 17r ph James Merrell/Andrew Arnott and Karin Shack's house in Melbourne; 18 ph Alan Williams/Lisa Fine's apartment in Paris; 19a ph James Merrell/antique curtains from Antiques and Things; 19bl ph Polly Wreford/The Sawmills Studios; 19bc ph James Merrell/fabric from Pierre Frey; 19br ph Polly Wreford/The Sawmills Studios; 20 both ph David Montgomery/Sabina Fay Braxton's apartment in Paris; 21al ph David Montgomery/Annabel Astor's house in London is full of furniture and accessories designed exclusively for her OKA Direct Mail order catalogue; 21ar ph James Merrell/Christophe Gollut's apartment in London; 21ac&b Christian de Falbe's London home; 22al ph Christopher Drake/Marisa Cavalli's home in Milan; 22ac ph James Merrell/fabric and bobble fringe from Jane Churchill; 22ar Debby & Jeremy Amias' house in London designed by Carden Cunietti; 23 ph Christopher Drake/Marisa Cavalli's home in Milan; 24al ph Jan Baldwin/Laurence & Yves Sabourets' house in Brittany; 24ar ph James Merrell/Janie Jackson-stylist/designer; 24bl ph Chris Everard/Eric De Queker's apartment in Antwerp; 24br Simon Upton; 25 ph Ray Main/a house in London designed by Mark Guard Architects; 26–27 Christian de Falbe's London home; 28 Designed by Steven Roxburghe; 28–29 ph James Merrell/an apartment in New York, architect Campion A. Platt; 29 ph James Merrell/Kelly Hoppen's apartment in London; 30a ph Tom Leighton; 30bl ph James Merrell/an apartment in New York designed by James Biber of Pentagram with curtain design by Mary Bright; 30br ph Chris Everard/Eric De Queker's apartment in Antwerp; 31a ph Ray Main/Nello Renault's loft in Paris; 31b ph David Montgomery/Sasha Waddell's house in London; 32 Debby & Jeremy Amias' house in London designed by Carden Cunietti; 33 Designed by Steven Roxburghe; 34 ph James Merrell/Vincent Dané's house near Biarritz; 34–35 ph James Merrell/Sue and Andy A'Court's apartment in Blackheath, London; 35 ph James Merrell/A house designed by Mary Drysdale; 36 & 39 a house in London designed by François Gilles & Dominique Lubar, IPL Interiors; 40a ph Simon Upton; 40b ph David Montgomery/Blakes Lodging designed by Jeanie Blake www.picket.com/blakesBB/blakes.htm; 41al&ar ph Simon Upton; 41bl ph Henry Bourne; 41br ph James Merrell/Frédéric Méchiche's home in Toulon; 42l ph Simon Upton; 42r both Anne-Mette Fiil's house near Cambridge; 43 ph James Merrell/fabrics from Housemade; 46 ph Simon Upton; 48 Sheila Scholes' house near Cambridge; 49 ph James Merrell/Nigel Greenwood's apartment in London; 50al ph James Merrell/antique linen from Nicole Fabre, curtains by Reed Creative Services; 50bl ph James Merrell/fabric from Cath Kidston; 50r ph James Merrell/Christophe Gollut's apartment in London; 51a ph James Merrell/Interni Interior Design Consultancy; 51b ph James Merrell/Andrew Parr's house in Melbourne; 52, 53 & 55 Emily Todhunter's house in London designed by Todhunter Earle Interiors; 56 Curtain design by Sian and Annie Colley; 57al ph James Merrell/muslin from JAB, pole made to order; 57bl ph Andrew Wood/Mary Shaw's Sequana apartment in Paris; 57r ph James Merrell/an apartment in London designed by Ash Sakula Architects; 58al ph Christopher Drake/Enrica Stabile's house in Brunello; 58bl&r ph James Merrell/fabric from Shaker, pole from Artisan; 59 & 61 ph James Merrell/Hotel Villa Gallici Aix en Provence, France; 62 ph James Merrell/an apartment in London designed by Charles Rutherfoord; 63a ph Alan Williams/Interior Designer and Managing Director of the Société Yves Halard, Michelle Halard's own apartment in Paris; 63bl ph Simon Upton; 63bc ph James Merrell/designed by Larcombe and Solomon; 63br ph James Merrell/Vincent Dané's house near Biarritz; 64 ph Simon Upton; 65 ph Chris Everard/Lisa & Richard Frisch's apartment in New York designed by Patricia Seidman of Mullman Seidman Architects; 66 ph James Merrell; 67l ph Debi Treloar/The Zwirner's loft in New York; 67ar ph Andrew Wood/ Brian Johnson's apartment in London designed by Johnson Naylor; 67cr ph David Montgomery/Sabina Fay Braxton's apartment in Paris; 67br ph Andrew Wood/Johanne Riss' house in Brussels; 68al ph Sandra Lane; 68ar ph Christopher Drake/Marisa Cavalli's home in Milan; 68bl ph Polly Wreford/ Kimberley Watson's house in London; 68br Anne-Mette Fiil's house near Cambridge; 69 main & inset left Anne-Mette Fiil's house near Cambridge; 69 inset centre ph Polly Wreford; 69 inset right ph Sandra Lane; 70 ph Simon Upton; 70–71 Anne-Mette Fiil's house near Cambridge; 71 Sheila Scholes' house near Cambridge; 72 ph James Merrell; 74all Christian de Falbe's London home; 75 both Debby & Jeremy Amias' house in London designed by Carden Cunietti; 76 ph James Merrell/sheer fabric from Sanderson, ribbon from V. V. Rouleaux, expansion rod from John Lewis; 78al ph Ray Main; 78bl ph Alan Williams/ Owner of Gloss, Pascale Bredillet's own apartment in London; 78ar ph James Merrell/fabric from Habitat, pole from McKinney & Co; 78br ph James Merrell/fabric, pole and fringe from John Lewis; 79 ph James Merrell/fabric from Pongees, ammonite knobs from John Lewis; 80 Debby & Jeremy Amias' house in London designed by Carden Cunietti; 81 ph James Merrell/architects, Ogawa Depardon, curtain designed by Mary Bright; 82al ph Sandra Lane; 82ac ph James Merrell/fabric from McKinney & Co, poles from Artisan, antique ring clips from Antiques & Things; 82ar ph James Merrell/ready-made curtains from The Source; 82b ph James Merrell/fabric from Sanderson, tension wire kit from Ikea; 83al Sheila Scholes' house near Cambridge; 83ac ph James Merrell/muslin from JAB, pole made to order; 83ar ph David Montgomery/designed by Todhunter Earle Interiors; 83bl ph Simon Upton; 83br ph James Merrell/both fabrics from KA International; 84 & 85 Sheila Scholes' house near Cambridge; 86al&bl ph James Merrell/Frédéric Méchiche's house near Toulon; 86acl ph Sandra Lane; 86acr ph James Merrell; 86ar ph Sandra Lane; 87a Christian de Falbe's London home; 87b Emily Todhunter's house in London designed by Todhunter Earle Interiors; 88 Curtain design by Sian and Annie Colley; 90 ph James Merrell/fabric from Sanderson, binding from John Lewis; 91al ph James Merrell/Khai & Sue Kellet; 91ac ph James Merrell/ fabric from F. R. Street, felt from Muraspec, pole from Artisan; 91ar ph James Merrell/designed by François Gilles and Dominique Lubar, IPL Interiors; 91b ph James Merrell/fabric and bobble fringe from Jane Churchill; 92 Sheila Scholes' house near Cambridge; 94 ph David Montgomery/Blakes Lodging designed by Jeanie Blake www.picket.com/blakesBB/blakes.htm; 96–97 A house in London designed by Charlotte Crosland Interiors; 98, 98–99 & 99a A house in London designed by Charlotte Crosland Interiors; 99c & 99b Curtain design by Sian and Annie Colley; 100 Sheila Scholes' house near Cambridge; 101l ph Chris Everard/An apartment in Milan designed by Nicoletta Marazza; 101ar ph James Merrell/Vicente Wolfe's apartment, New York; 101cr Curtain design by Sian and Annie Colley; 101br ph Andrew Wood/Roger & Fay Oates' house in Eastnor; 102 ph Henry Bourne; 104 ph James Merrell/fabric from F. R. Street, felt from Muraspec, pole from Artisan; 104–105 & 105a Curtain design by Sian and Annie Colley; 105b A house in London designed by Charlotte Crosland Interiors; 106–107 & 109 Debby & Jeremy Amias' house in London designed by Carden Cunietti; 110–111 A house in London designed by Charlotte Crosland Interiors; 112l ph Ray Main/Malin Iovino's apartment in London; 112ar ph Christopher Drake/ Enrica Stabile's house in Milano; 112br ph James Merrell/ Vincent Dané's house near Biarritz; 113 Curtain design by Sian and Annie Colley; 114l ph Ray Main/Nello Renault's loft in Paris; 114ar ph James Merrell; 114br ph Henry Bourne; 115 & 117 ph Simon Upton; 118al ph Ray Main; 118ar ph David Montomery/The House of Crypton living laboratory apartment showroom in New York City designed by CR Studio Architects, PC; 118bl Emily Todhunter's house in London designed by Todhunter Earle Interiors; 118br & 119 A house in London designed by Charlotte Crosland Interiors; 120–121 A house in London designed by François Gilles and Dominique Lubar of IPL Interiors; 122 ph David Montgomery/ Sasha Waddell's house in London; 123 ph Sandra Lane; 124 A house in London designed by François Gilles and Dominique Lubar of IPL Interiors; 125 Emily Todhunter's house in London designed by Todhunter Earle Interiors; 126 ph Debi Treloar/ Victoria Andreae's house in London;128a ph Christopher Drake/Enrica Stabile's house in Le Thor; 128bl Emily Todhunter's house in London designed by Todhunter Earle Interiors; 128br ph Christopher Drake/Diane Bauer's house near Cotignac; 129 ph Debi Treloar/Victoria Andreae's house in London; 130al ph Simon Upton; 130ar & 130bl Debby & Jeremy Amias' house in London designed by Carden Cunietti; 130br & 131 A house in London designed by François Gilles and Dominique Lubar of IPL Interiors;132l Debby & Jeremy Amias' house in London designed by Carden Cunietti; 132r ph Catherine Gratwicke/Jeff McKay's apartment in New York; 133 ph Sandra Lane; 138 Debby & Jeremy Amias' house in London designed by Carden Cunietti; 140 Sheila Scholes' house near Cambridge; 143 Designed by Steven Roxburghe; 144 Sheila Scholes' house near Cambridge.

In addition to the designers and home owners mentioned above we would also like to thank the following: Nancy Braithwaite, Mr & Mrs Derald Ruttenberg; Beverly Jacomini, Wendy Harrop, Bruno & Hélène Lafforgue, Marie Kalt, Lena Proudlock, Liz Dougherty Pierce, K Russell Glover & Angela Miller and Tricia Foley.

INDEX

Figures in *italics* indicate captions; those in **bold** indicate projects.

ACKNOWLEDGMENTS

This book is the product of the considerable talents of the creative team put
together by Ryland Peters & Small. I would like to thank, in particular, Alison for
asking me to be involved in the first place; Sophie for her patience, editorial
guidance and eye for detail; Emily for the faultless picture research; Ali for her
elegant prose, and especially Lizzie for her exquisite watercolours.

Lucinda Ganderton